NEEDLEPOINT
—LACE—
Designs from the Town

NEEDLEPOINT
—LACE—
Designs from the Town

Doreen Holmes

B.T. Batsford Ltd • London

This book is dedicated to my family
and especially to the memory of my
Dad.

First published 1994

Printed in Singapore

Published by
B.T. Batsford Ltd
4 Fitzhardinge Street
London W1H 0AH

A catalogue record for this book is available
from the British Library

ISBN 0 7134 7178 6

Contents

Dolphin and Girl, designed and worked by the author (see p. 81)

Preface

At first glance towns do not seem very likely places to inspire the needlelacer. There is, however, a wealth of material to use if only you know where and how to look, and this book is intended to help you do just that. Even the most ordinary and boring things in the town can be used to produce pleasing designs: Victorian brick patterns, manhole covers and wrought-iron railings to name but a few. The buildings and people can also provide just the right inspiration when you see them with the eyes of a needlelacer, and I hope that, having read this book, you will begin to look beneath the surface of the town. As in my previous book, *Designs from the Countryside*, the stitches and colours are purely suggestions to help those of you who need a starting-off point, but I do hope that you will soon begin to make the designs your own.

Acknowledgements

I should like to thank all my family and friends who have helped in the making of this book: my husband Keith Holmes for the photography; my son Tim and daughter Sally for their expertise on the computer; my friends Pat Gibson, Nina Devereux, Hilary Roberts, Molly Buckle, Barbara Netherwood, Rita Baldwin, Cynthia Brockhouse, Margaret Reeves, Julia White and Maureen Long for their needlelace; Iris Wallbank and Leonie Phipps for their designing ability; Barbara Hirst for teaching me how to do stumpwork; the Weald and Downland Open Air Museum at Singleton for allowing us to photograph the Market Hall; and, of course, the lady to whom I owe it all, Nenia Lovesey.

People

1 *The Tramp, designed and worked by Nina Devereux*

1

The Tramp

MATERIALS NEEDED

Gutermann pure silk 100/3:
    Nos 446, 979 and 769 (brown)
    38, 40 and 783 (grey)
    810 (purple)
    000 (black)
    658 (flesh)
    802 (cream)

STITCHES USED

Corded Brussels and Twisted Buttonhole

INSTRUCTIONS

Stage 1: The Hat
Using Corded Brussels stitch throughout
(unless otherwise stated), work the small torn
piece in black and the main part in mid-grey,
cream and black (working from **a** to **b**). You
will need to use the vertical shading to create
the light effect on the right-hand side of the
hat. Incorporate a black cord or a line of black
stitches now and again to add interest.

Stage 2: The Face and Hair
The top part of the face above the eyes is
worked in purple to give the shadow effect; the
rest of the face is worked in flesh colour. The
eyes, nose and mouth are worked on top
afterwards as cordonnettes. The underside of
the chin and the neck are worked in purple to
create shadow. The hair can be worked in one
piece over the cordonnets and the cordonnettes put on afterwards; this is much easier
and neater.

1 pattern

Stage 3: The Jacket

Arm **c** is worked in two greys, the lighter one being used for the upper arm, with a mixture of the two for the lower part. The creases at the bend of the arm are cordonnettes, worked afterwards. The collar of the jacket is a mixture of purple and black, using the latter for the shadow under the edge of the collar. The jacket is then worked across from **d** to **e**, using black under the collar, light grey on the shoulder and top of the sleeve, and mid-grey further down the jacket. Add a purple cord where the shadow falls under the arm and towards the bottom of the jacket. The pocket is worked without the triangular flap, which is then worked separately, leaving loose ends when working the cordonnette in order to give a tattered look. Sew the flap on afterwards. Use flesh coloured thread to work the hand, wrist, knees and the small piece of elbow which shows through.

Stage 4: The Trousers

These are worked lengthways, using the brown of the lamppost for the leg that is behind and dark grey, black and purple for the one in front. The horizontal shading technique is used here, adding each new colour as a cord and working from the dark grey on the right through to purple on the left edge.

Stage 5: The Lamppost

This is worked lengthways, using brown for the bottom section as far as the hand, then black for the rest. The rings at the bottom and in the centre are worked horizontally. The stitch used is a combination of Corded Brussels and Twisted stitch.

Stage 6: The Dog

Begin at **a** and work a short row of two or three stitches in cream. Increase the length of the row each time, taking the third or fourth row into the snout so that the rows curve upwards, making the dog look up. Change to the mid-colour and continue curving the rows slightly until the bottom of the jaw is reached. Continue shorter rows for a little longer down the ear, then open this out into rows of Twisted stitch to the bottom of the ear.

The dog's neck is worked lengthways from **b** to **c**, using a lighter cord and dark-brown stitches. The back ear is worked in dark-brown Twisted stitch. The bib under the collar is worked in the tan colour, beginning with a close Twisted stitch and opening out towards the bottom of the bib. The rest of the chest is in dark brown, down to the tops of the legs; these are worked lengthways, using a combination of tan and dark brown. The back of the body is also worked in this way. For the cordonnette use the colour of the adjacent stitches. The eye is worked as a tiny cordonnette afterwards, and the dog's lead is a light-coloured cordonnette which is allowed to twist all the way up and end in a fringed tassel.

The Lamplighter

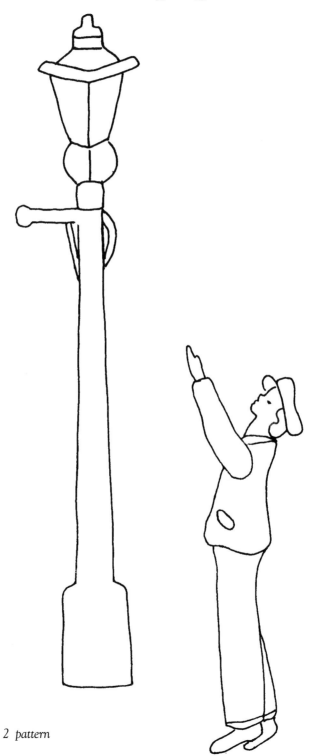

2 pattern

MATERIALS NEEDED

Gutermann pure silk 100/3:
   Nos 8 and 701 (light and dark grey)
   000 (black)
   800 (white)
   658 (flesh colour)
   180 (brown) for the hair

STITCHES USED

Corded Brussels

INSTRUCTIONS

Stage 1: The Lamppost

This is worked in black Corded Brussels with the light being worked as a cordonnette only. A white cord has been added towards the bottom half of the lamp standard to give some reflection.

Stage 2: The Man

The man is worked in Corded Brussels, using the two greys for his clothes. A striped effect is achieved by alternating the colour of cord and stitches, i.e. light cord/dark stitches – light cord/light stitches – dark cord/light stitches, etc. His shoes are of black stitches over a light cord and his hat comprises dark-grey stitches bordered by a black cordonnette. Use a flesh colour for his hand and face, and stitch the small eye on afterwards.

Stage 3: Mounting

If you mount The Lamplighter onto a piece of card you can easily colour the background with pencils to show the shaft of light. Stick the sequins into the lamp to add sparkle and use a piece of wire or a cocktail stick for his lighter.

2 The Lamplighter, designed by Nina Devereux and worked by Hilary Roberts

3

The Flower Seller

3 The Flower Seller, designed by Iris Wallbank and worked by the author

MATERIALS NEEDED

Gutermann pure silk 100/3:
  Nos 000 (black)
  817 (brown)
  802 (off-white)
A selection of colours for the flowers
Brown covered wire
Fine wire for hands and arm
Clear glue
Silver thread for the brooch
Dark felt
Small piece of linen for the underskirt
Unwashed calico for the background
Embroidery frame

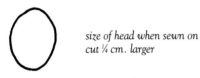

size of head when sewn on cut ¼ cm. larger

3 head

3a basic body shape

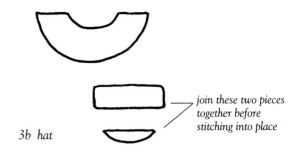

join these two pieces together before stitching into place

3b hat

STITCHES USED

Corded Brussels, Four Pin buds, Twisted and Shell

INSTRUCTIONS

Background

Using a light box (or the window) trace the outline of the flower seller onto the calico with a blue (water soluble) pencil. Paint your background, using either silk paints or ordinary watercolours. Stretch your calico over an embroidery frame and paint in the required background.

Stage 1: The Face

Make the face and stitch into place (see p. 119).

Stage 2: The Body

Stitch a dark felt onto the body shape, using stab stitches and putting on extra layers to make the contours. Note that only parts of the arms need to be padded with felt (down as far as the elbow each time) because her left forearm comes out to hold the bunch of flowers, and her right forearm will be padded after the skirt and shawl have been stitched on.

Stage 3: The Clothes

THE UNDERSKIRT may be added if you wish; I made one from a piece of linen and left it with a plain edge, but alternatively a small picot edge may be worked using Shell stitch. Stitch this at the waist and down each side of the skirt shape.

THE BODICE is simply that part which shows at

neck edge – Shell stitch edging

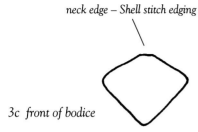

3c front of bodice

the neck. Work this in brown Corded Brussels and stitch into place, with Shell stitch around the neck to make a high-necked dress. A silver brooch may be added, using silver thread and a very fine needle.

THE SKIRT is worked in Corded Brussels, using the dark brown and black in alternate vertical stripes. Work a cordonnette along the bottom edge only. Take it off its backing and stitch into place, concealing your stab stitches under the edge of the body. Ease into place at the waistline, gathering very slightly if necessary.

3d skirt (underskirt the same size but in material)

THE APRON is worked in Corded Brussels with a Twisted stitch edge round three sides (not the waist edge). Having worked the Twisted stitch, take the cord all the way back by hooking it into each loop, then work lengthways down the apron, putting two stitches into every loop and hooking into the

Twisted stitch along the bottom edge each time. Incorporate Four Pin buds at intervals along the bottom.

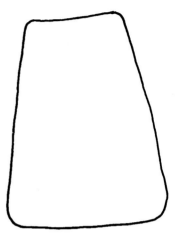

3e apron

THE SHAWL. Work shawl **a** in black Corded Brussels and fringe the bottom edge by knotting two threads into approximately every third loop. A cordonnette should be worked along the front edge. Stitch into place along the outside edge of the body, down as far as the elbow of that arm and along the front edge of the shawl as far as the waist.

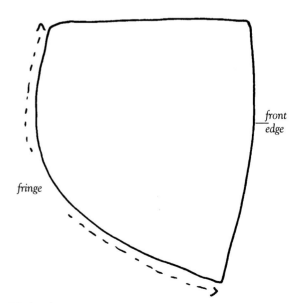

fringe

front edge

*3f shawl **a***

Work shawl **b** in the same way. When stitching on, fold and tuck to give the effect of a full shawl.

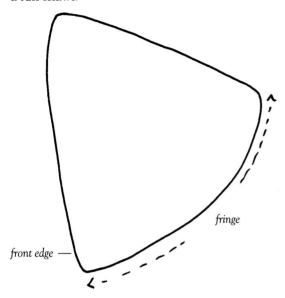

front edge —

fringe

3g shawl **b**

Stage 4: The Arms

Hook up the shawl on the flower seller's right side, to suggest the position of the arm, and stitch felt into place for the forearm of her right arm. Work a piece of brown Corded Brussels separately, making it slightly larger than the felt shape and with a Shell stitch edging at the wrist. Stitch into place over the felt forearm. Do not stitch down at the wrist because this is where the hand must be inserted.

The other forearm is made with a bundle of

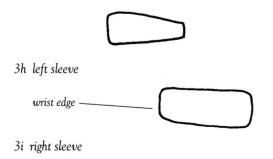

3h left sleeve

wrist edge ———

3i right sleeve

wires. Twist them together and wrap with tissue until you have the required size. At the elbow end, cut off some of the excess wire and push the remaining two or three strands through the calico at the bottom of the upper arm. Twist these wires at the back and stitch down so that the arm comes out at the right angle. Make a piece of brown Corded Brussels for the sleeve; this must be large enough to go all the way round the arm. Stitch round the arm and then stitch at the elbow.

Stage 5: The Hands

Make two hands (see instructions on p. 119), being careful to make one right and one left! Push the wires of each hand into their respective arms. If you feel happier, put a small amount of clear glue onto the wires before you push them in.

Stage 6: The Hat

Work the two pieces of crown first as black Corded Brussels, sew them together then stitch into place, putting in extra wadding if necessary. Work the lace for the brim. Work the cordonnette along the outside edge of the brim, laying in wire and leaving extra at each end. Push the two ends of the wire through the calico on each side of the hat. Twist these wires at the back and sew down securely. Make a few flowers to decorate the hat.

Stage 7: The Basket

Collect together an even number of wires (approximately ten) about 7½ cm. in length. Tie these in a bundle with a short length of wire and add some glue to make sure they are really fastened. Splay out the wires, pushing the centre bundle downwards; this will make the other wires curve up into a large bowl shape. Take a new piece of wire and begin weaving your basket from the centre; keep stroking the wires upwards. The centre fastening will be inside the finished basket. Continue weaving until the appropriate size is reached; fasten off the top of the basket by weaving each of the spokes in front of two and behind one all round the top. Tuck in the last piece of wire. Bend the basket into the shape you require, remembering that the glued wires are on the inside.

Make the handle by bending two wires in half. Thread two through the top edge of the basket, twist all four wires together, then take two wires through the opposite edge. Cut off the other two then bend back the two that have been threaded through, onto the handle, and twist until fastened.

Stage 8: The Flowers
These are described under *Basic Couronne* (Stage 3) on p. 116. Make enough to fill the basket and a few extra for the bunch in the flower seller's hand. Glue those for the basket into place. Wire the bunch together and fit into her hand.

To make the delphiniums, thread your needle, tie the thread onto fine wire, then wrap the thread round two or three times. Bend the wire over so that the knot is in the bend. Wind the thread round both wires, making French knots into it as you go. Fasten off with a half-hitch.

Stage 9: The Feet
Cut two small cup shapes out of the dark felt for the toe of each shoe; sew into place.

4

Yeoman of the Guard

MATERIALS NEEDED

Gutermann pure silk 100/3:
   Nos. 156 (red)
   416 (yellow)
   000 (black)
   800 (white)
   658 (flesh)
Madeira 40 No. 483:
   Gold thread (small amount)
   Blue thread (small amount)
Soft black leather (small amount)
Double sided Sellotape
2 mm. graph paper
Wire for the staff
Tin foil (small amount)
Unwashed calico fabric for background
Felt for padding
Embroidery frame

INSTRUCTIONS

Background
Paint the background using watercolour
paints. I painted two basic tower shapes and a
portcullis, plus an area of grey to represent
paving stones. When everything was finished,
I drew in the details with coloured pencils.
Using a light box, I finally traced the outline
of the figure onto the calico in the appropriate
place.

Stage 1: The Face
Make a face and stitch onto the calico. Work
the hair, using a dark brown, and stitch the
ears into place, using bullion knots.

Stage 2: The Body
Stitch felt onto the body shape, leaving a

*take the head shape from here
and remember to leave a slight
space under the chin for the
ruff to sit in*

4 basic shape

small space under the chin; this is where the
ruff fits in. Add an extra layer of felt to the
chest area.

Stage 3: The Clothes
These are worked in Corded Brussels
throughout.

THE SKIRT. The two pieces are worked in the
same way. Lay down the cordonnette in
yellow. Work two rows of black all the way
round the edge, then two rows of yellow, four
rows of red, two yellow, two black and two
yellow. Fill in the middle section with red,
working along the length and hooking into
the existing stitches.

Work a yellow cordonnette as shown in

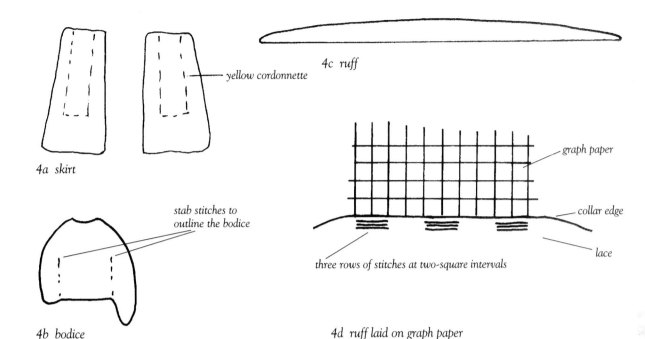

4a skirt

yellow cordonnette

4c ruff

graph paper

collar edge

lace

three rows of stitches at two-square intervals

stab stitches to outline the bodice

4b bodice

4d ruff laid on graph paper

diagram 4a, laying down two threads and catching the stitches underneath. Repeat in black on the inside of the shape, and again in yellow. Put the bars across this small centre section, using a Twisted stitch each time. Work a yellow cordonnette along the bottom edge; *do not work a cordonnette along the sides or at the waist.* Take each piece off its backing and sew into position at the waist and down each side. Make sure that your stab stitches disappear under the edge of the skirt.

THE BODICE. The lace for his right arm is shorter than the full length of the arm, because an extra piece will be fitted later. Work the bodice in red; *do not work cordonnettes.* Stitch into place, remembering to leave a space under the chin. Once in position, stab stitch a line between the chest and the arms to create an indentation on each side.

Sew the braids from the shoulders to the waist, using long stitches: two yellow, two black and two yellow. Do the same with the braids on the sleeves but make only one stitch each time instead of two. Sew on the crown, thistle, etc.,

using ordinary stitches and French knots; add a stitch of gold here and there.

THE BELT. Stick some double-sided Sellotape to a piece of paper. Lay threads onto the tape in this order: two black, two yellow, one black, three red, one black, two yellow, two black. Cut the belt to the required length; glue each end and stick into place. Sew on the buckle, using yellow thread and taking it under the belt each time.

THE MEDALS. Cut a tiny piece of card and stick double-sided Sellotape to one side; this will help to fix the thread. Wind the Madeira thread round the card, and when it is covered take the thread through the back to fasten off. Stick this in place, then work French knots along the bottom edge.

THE RUFF. Work this in Corded Brussels with a Twisted stitch edge along the straight side. Work a cordonnette along the straight edge, laying down two extra threads. Take the lace from its backing and lay onto 2 mm. graph paper. To hold the lace in place, fix at each end by sticking onto double-sided Sellotape.

4 *Yeoman of the Guard, designed and worked by the author*

Mark off in two square sections, as shown in diagram 4d. Make three rows of straight stitches along the shaped edge, using three separate pieces of thread so that they can be pulled up. Take the lace off the paper and gather up. Using the gathering threads, sew the ruff into position around the chin. The tapered edges should make the ruff look as if it is disappearing behind the head.

THE HAT. Make the crown of the hat first, in black Corded Brussels. Stitch into place, adding more wadding if necessary. Make the brim and lay wire down as you work the cordonnette along the outside edge. Take this from the backing and push the wires through the calico on each side of the hat; stitch the two pieces together. Twist the wires at the back and fasten. Sew French knots around the crown of the hat in red, white and blue.

4e hat

Stage 4: The Legs
Work two pieces of Corded Brussels and stitch into place. Cut two shoes out of the leather and stitch on. Sew red, white and blue French knots round a centre of red loops on the top of each shoe.

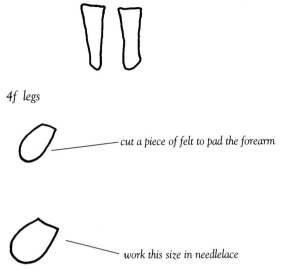

4f legs

cut a piece of felt to pad the forearm

work this size in needlelace

4g forearm

Stage 5: The Left Forearm
Stitch a small piece of felt into place for the forearm (two pieces if you think it needs more padding), then work a piece of lace large enough to cover this. Sew the lace into place down each side of the arm but leave the wrist end open. Make a hand, with fingers clenched to hold the staff, and push this into the wrist opening.

Stage 6: The Staff
Take a piece of brown covered wire and make a loop at the top, covering this with tin foil. Then add tiny marks with a black felt-tip pen. If you do not have any covered wire, use ordinary wire and cover with the basic Brussels stitch, working the stitches very close together so that the wire cannot be seen. Put the staff into the left hand.

Buildings

5 La Bequinage, worked by the author

5

La Bequinage

5 pattern

MATERIALS NEEDED

Dragonfly 140 (formerly Unity 50)
Gutermann 100/3 white silk

STITCHES USED

Pea, Williamson, Corded, Double Corded,
Single Brussels, Twisted and Water

INSTRUCTIONS

Stage 1
The side and the front of the house are
worked in Corded Brussels as are the chimneys
and the gateway. The rows for the side of the
house begin at the apex of the roof with two
stitches; lengthen the rows as you work. The
gateway is worked lengthways. All other areas
are worked in horizontal rows. The roof is in
Williamson stitch.

Stage 2
The wall at the side of the house is in Twisted
stitch with thread woven in and out
afterwards to create texture.

Stage 3
The trees are worked in Pea stitch and Double
Corded Brussels.

Stage 4
The bridge has a guard rail of Twisted stitch,
and the bridge support is worked in Corded
Brussels; the under-arch areas are in Single
Brussels, which allows the background colour
to show through, thus creating shadow.

Stage 5
The canal is worked in Water stitch. The
cordonnette is worked in the usual way.

6

New York Skyline

MATERIALS NEEDED

Gutermann pure silk 100/3 in black
Madeira no. 15 in gold (22)
Madeira metallic nos 40, 251

STITCHES USED

Williamson, Pea, Corded Brussels, Ardenza bars, Cinq Point de Venise and Shell stitch variation

INSTRUCTIONS

All the shaded areas are worked in black or gold Corded Brussels, and all areas are worked lengthways unless otherwise stated.

Sections **a** and **j** are worked in black Williamson stitch.

Sections **c**, **r** and **u** are worked in alternate rows of black and gold Corded Brussels.

Section **d** is worked in gold Pea stitch.

Sections **f** and **w** are Williamson stitch, using the Madeira metallic 251.

Sections **h** and **q** are metallic 251 Corded Brussels.

Sections **k** and **z** are worked in Shell stitch variation, using the gold thread for the row of shells.

Sections **n** and **g** are gold Corded Brussels.

Sections **l** and **y** are worked in gold and black Corded Brussels, one row gold, two black.

Sections **m**, **s** and **za** are worked using the gold thread as the cord and black for the stitches.

Section **p** is gold Williamson stitch.

The steps at the top of section **x** are filled with Ardenza bars, as are sections **zd**.

Sections **zb** are black Williamson stitch but worked horizontally.

Section **zc** is black Pea stitch.

The cordonnette is worked mainly in black but the areas worked only in gold have a gold cordonnette; work with one strand of the gold thread and lay down the remaining two.

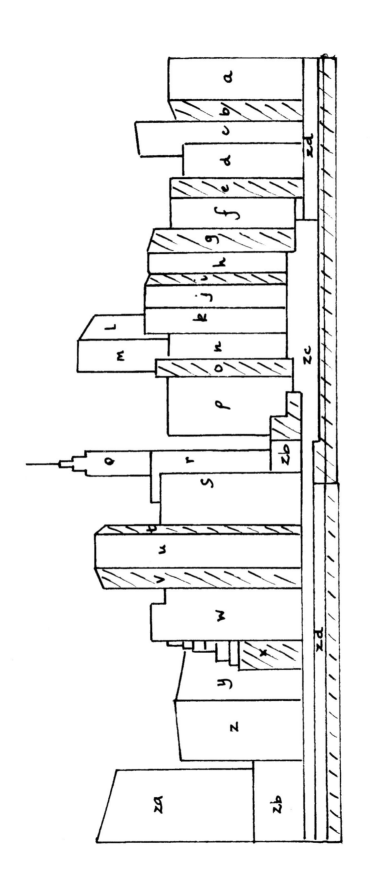

6 pattern

6 New York Skyline, designed and worked by the author

7

The Apothecary's Shop

MATERIALS NEEDED

Glue
Double-sided Sellotape
Unwashed calico and circular embroidery
    frame
Clear plastic
Thin card (small amount)
Soft leather (small amount)
Silk dyes
Cocktail stick
Wire to support window frame and blind
Balsa wood
Wadding (small amount)
A blue pencil which will wash off fabric, such
    as a Madeira Handcraft (water-eraseable)
    marker
Gutermann pure silk 100/3
    Nos 701, 224 for the stones
    5, 258, 722, 994 for the blind
    414 for the windows and doors
    931, 585, 271, 582 for leaves and bushes
    910, 327 for flowers
Madeira metallic thread 40:
    Nos 38, 28 and 57 (blue, rust and green)

N.B. All the needlelace is worked separately
onto a foundation material in the usual way.

INSTRUCTIONS

Stage 1: Preparation

Using a light box or windowpane, place the
tracing of your pattern underneath the calico
and draw onto the material with the blue pen.
Stretch your calico flat and, using a paintbrush
and water, dampen the outside of your pattern.
Drop the dye onto the material and it will

7 basic pattern

spread over the damp area. You will always
have a hard line where the water stops – the
colour will run only to the outside edges of the
watered area. Use grey towards the bottom of
the shop, merging into green at the sides and
blue at the top. Wash blue onto the areas
where there are windows and use stone colour
for the stones on the walls. Put this prepared
material into your circular embroidery frame
and pull until taut.

Stage 2: Stones

Work these in the normal way, varying the
colour and size. Shading could be used to give
added depth to the lintels over the windows

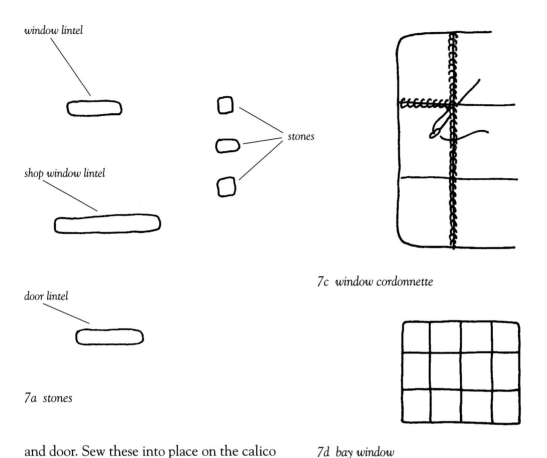

window lintel

stones

shop window lintel

door lintel

7a stones

7c window cordonnette

7d bay window

and door. Sew these into place on the calico shape. Some of the very tiny stones may be worked as a cordonnette straight onto the calico.

Stage 3: Windows
The top two windows are laid down as a cordonnet and worked as a simple cordonnette: work the vertical lines first and the horizontal lines afterwards, threading the needle each time under the vertical line already worked. The bay window is worked in the same way but with the horizontal lines worked first and the vertical ones afterwards.

The outside edge has wire included so that the window may be 'bowed' into position. To create this bow, two small bowed pieces of balsa wood or card need to be cut and glued to the base calico, one for the top of the window and one for the sill.

The curtain is worked separately and stitched onto a cocktail stick before being sewn into place. The bottles are worked separately and then sewn onto the curtain.

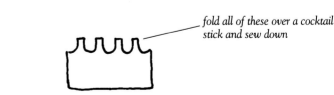

fold all of these over a cocktail stick and sew down

7b window

7e curtain for shop window

7f bottle

Stage 4: The Blind

This is worked in the usual way in stripes of colour with a Twisted stitch vein down the centre of each stripe. Wire is included in the cordonnette along the bottom edge; *no other cordonnettes are worked.* Two rows of looped edging are worked along the front using the two colours; work one row as you are working the cordonnette, then work the second row on top.

direction
of stitches

7g blind

7h scalloped edging for the blind

Stage 5: The Window Boxes

Measure the bottom width of the window, then cut a piece of card the same length plus an extra piece at each end for the sides of the box. You will also need small flaps to tuck

these two end flaps stick to the calico when folded in

score along the dotted lines cut along the full lines

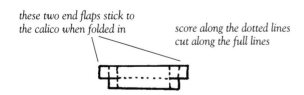

7i window box

behind and stick to the calico. Cover the front and sides of the box with a soft leather or a strip of needlelace in the appropriate colour. Stick the boxes into place and sew with one or two stitches through the calico.

Stage 6 : Flowers

These are worked as shown, using the same technique as for a couronne but working the stitches on the inside of the circle rather than the outside. Sew these into the window boxes through the calico.

Stage 7: The Door

This is worked using Corded Brussels stitch and the no. 414 thread. The black hinges and the doorknob are embroidered on afterwards when the door has been removed from its backing material and stitched into place. The shading in this instance was done with Karisma pencils.

The doorstep is made by binding two pieces of card, one slightly larger than the other. Put double-sided Sellotape along one side of the card then bind with thread; the tape helps to hold the thread in place. Stick the steps into position.

7j door

mark in the tiles with long stitches add shading with coloured pencils

7k roof

7 *The Apothecary's Shop, designed by Leonie Phipps and worked by the author*

Stage 8: The Roof

This is worked using a pale-grey colour. Work the cordonnette all the way round and remove from the backing material. Sew this into place on the shop. Use a dark-grey silk for the long stitches on the slates. The shading was again put on with Karisma pencils.

Stage 9: The Chimney

A small piece of Corded Brussels is needed for the bottom of the chimney. When this is sewn into place, stuff slightly, then stitch two chimney pots onto the calico at the top of the padded section, using satin stitch. Karisma pencils can be used for the shading.

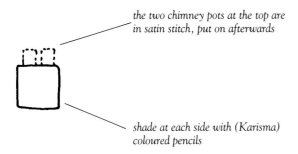

the two chimney pots at the top are in satin stitch, put on afterwards

shade at each side with (Karisma) coloured pencils

7l chimney

Stage 10 : Bushes

These are simply French knots worked onto a separate piece of calico. This is then cut out with approximately ½ cm. of calico to spare at the edge. Place running stitches round the edge and gather up, adding a small amount of stuffing at this stage. Sew into place.

As I have already said painting is the traditional way to deal with the background but you can use the Karisma pencils, which are sufficiently soft to blend well on calico. However, if pencils are used then the background must be added last of all, otherwise the pencil may smudge onto the lace.

If you would like to know more about stumpwork see Barbara and Roy Hirst's book *Raised Embroidery: A Practical Guide to Decorative Stumpwork* (Merehurst).

Order of Mounting (Summary)

The stones should be stitched in place first, then the lintels over the windows and door. The top windows come next; place the plastic shape underneath the window frame then stitch the frame down. The bay window also needs a piece of plastic cut to the correct size. Sew the curtain and bottles in place, lay on the plastic so that the edges bow round the balsa wood, then lay on the frame and stitch into place. Now attach the door and stick the two pieces on to make the step. Glue and sew the window boxes, then sew in the flowers. Sew the roof and chimney in place, followed by the blind, and then sew on the bushes and stitch in the grass.

Take your picture out of the embroidery frame and put onto a piece of stiff card (laced at the back) ready to frame.

Street Scene

MATERIALS NEEDED

Gutermann pure silk 100/3:
  Nos 914 and 931 (greens)
  40 (grey)
  610, 5 and 802 (cream)
  221 (rust)
  612 (tan)
  817 and 439 (brown)
  000 (black)
  898 (dull gold)
  658 (flesh)
A small amount of red for the roses round the
  door

STITCHES USED

Corded and Double Corded Brussels

work this as a complete
shape – add Bullion
knots afterwards

8 pieman

INSTRUCTIONS

Stage 1: House 1
The houses are quite straightforward as
Corded Brussels is the only stitch used. The
walls of this house are worked horizontally and

8a house 1

in no. 914. The shutters are in no. 931 but this time worked vertically. The bars for the windowpanes are cordonnettes worked in the same colour as the shutters, but you must be careful not to put too many stitches in or the cordonnettes will begin to buckle. The roof is in no. 40 and worked across; the two small chimney pots are in no. 221. An extra cordonnette may be worked immediately under the roof line, in a dark colour, as guttering; this may also be incorporated in house 2. The door is worked in the same green as the shutters, leaving the centre panels empty so that the background colour can show through.

The cordonnettes are worked in the usual way, making sure that you work those for the shutters after those for the windows.

Stage 2: House 2 (see p. 38)
This house is worked in cream (no. 610) with no. 817 for the windows. The door is black and the roof is in rust (no. 221). The roses are stitched on afterwards.

Stage 3: House 3
No. 612 is used for this house, with no. 221 for the shutters and no. 817 for the window struts and door. A cordonnette of the rust colour has been worked on top of the stitches as panels for the door. The windows are smaller than those of the other houses, and could be worked as large Twisted stitches put in afterwards.

Stage 4: Bollards and Tree (see p. 38)
The bollards are in black Corded Brussels, and the tree is worked in the darker green and Corded Brussels. However, it could easily be

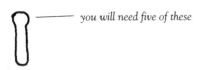

you will need five of these

8b bollard

8c house 3

worked in a more textured stitch such as Pea or Cinq Point de Venise. The trunk is brown Corded Brussels.

Stage 5: The Pie Man (see p. 38)
The pie man is worked in Corded Brussels throughout, apart from his basket, which is in Double Corded Brussels (no. 898); the handle has a twisted cordonnette.

His apron is in no. 802, worked lengthways. His trousers are in no. 817 and the top of his body no. 439. His hands and face are in the flesh colour and the tray of pies is a tray of Bullion knots on a cordonnette of brown. His cap is also in the darker brown.

The pavement and road are simply coloured paper with detail added in pencil.

8d tree

8e house 2

8 *Street Scene, designed by the author and worked by Rita Baldwin (the pieman), Cynthia Brockhouse (the tree), Maureen Long (house 2), Margaret Reeves (house 1) and Julia White (house 3), most of whom were beginners at needlelace*

St Basil's Cathedral, Moscow

MATERIALS NEEDED

Gutermann pure silk 100/3, nos 587, 931, 914,
  37, 435, 802, 8, 528 and 898
Gutermann Colour Collection, Sunset (no.
  245) and DMC Fil or Clair (gold thread)

STITCHES USED

Pea, Williamson, Twisted, Cinq Point de
Venise, Pea stitch variation 2, Alençon beads,
Single and Corded Brussels

9 pattern

INSTRUCTIONS

N.B. The cathedral should be made in one piece, using the pattern on p. 39; the diagrams showing individual towers are for reference only.

Lay the cordonnet in the usual way, using a neutral colour in the 100/3 silk. The crosses at the tops of the domes are worked as a gold cordonnette; the balls and the small sections underneath are also worked in one strand of the gold thread and Corded Brussels. The cordonnettes are in gold, laying in two extra threads.

Stage 1: Tower A

The dome is worked in Pea stitch, using colours 898 and 914 alternately. If you would like to shade to give a rounded effect, use the darker colours 528 and 931 for one row on the edges of each section. The cordonnettes are worked in the darker colour each time. The cordonnette at the bottom of the dome is in no. 802.

The next section down is worked in no. 587 and Corded Brussels. The bottom cordonnette has a scalloped edge, and another scalloped cordonnette in no. 931 is worked on top of the stitches halfway up this area. The area underneath is in no. 587 and Single Brussels with a cordonnette of the same colour.

The zigzag section (including the zigzag cordonnettes) is also in no. 587 and vertical cordonnettes have been added afterwards in no. 802.

The hoops have an edge of Twisted stitch in no. 587, plus one row of Corded Brussels; the rest of the hoop and the cordonnette are in no. 802. The small sections between the hoops are in no. 931.

The next three narrow sections are worked as follows:

1 Alençon beads and top cordonnette in no. 802.

2 Twisted stitch edge and top cordonnette in no. 931, plus one row of Corded Brussels; the rest is in no. 587 Corded Brussels.

3 Corded Brussels and top cordonnette: 587.

The bottom zigzag section is worked in no. 587 and Corded Brussels with the cordonnettes as shown in diagram 9a. The last section is in the Colour Collection thread in Corded Brussels; the cordonnettes are the same colour.

Stage 2: Tower B

The dome is worked in corded Brussels, using nos 37 and 802 alternately. To create depth, use no. 8 with no. 802, and no. 435 with no. 37, as shading along the edges. The cordonnettes are worked in the darker colours.

The section directly under the dome is worked

Pea stitch

extra picots and cordonnettes laid down on top of stitches (587 and 802)

cordonnette in 802

row of Twisted stitch in 587, then Corded Brussels in 802

row of Twisted stitch in 931, plus one row of Corded Brussels

cordonnette in 587

cordonnette in 802

9a tower A

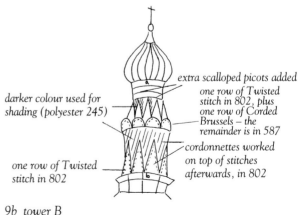

darker colour used for shading (polyester 245)

one row of Twisted stitch in 802

extra scalloped picots added one row of Twisted stitch in 802, plus one row of Corded Brussels – the remainder is in 587

cordonnettes worked on top of stitches afterwards, in 802

9b tower B

in one strand of the gold thread; the cordonnette is also in gold. The next band is in no. 587 and Corded Brussels with the cordonnette the same colour. The section below this has a Twisted stitch edge and a cordonnette in no. 931; the rest of the space is in no. 587 and Corded Brussels. Along this bottom cordonnette a scalloped edge has been added in no. 802.

The zigzag section is in Corded Brussels, using no. 587 and the Colour Collection thread, as shown in diagram 9c. The cordonnettes are worked in the colour of the adjacent stitches.

Colour Collection 245   Pure Silk 587

9c   zigzags (tower B)

The hoops have a Twisted stitch edge and cordonnette plus one row of Corded Brussels. The rest is in no. 587 and Corded Brussels. Extra interest may be added by using no. 802 as a cord for one or two rows after the Twisted stitch edge. Small couronnes in no. 587 are added afterwards. The cordonnette at the bottom of the hoops is in no. 931.

The next zigzag section is in Corded Brussels but with a Twisted stitch edging in no. 802 inside the triangular shapes, which are in no. 587. The top section is worked in the Colour Collection thread with cordonnettes worked in no. 802 on top of the stitches, as shown in diagram 9b.

The band below the zigzag section is in no. 931 and Pea stitch with the same colour cordonnette, and the last area is worked in no. 587 and Corded Brussels with cordonnettes of the same colour.

Stage 3: Tower C
The dome is worked in Cinq Point de Venise, using nos 587 and 931. Work a row of Cinq Point de Venise from left to right and fasten off. Join in the other colour at the left-hand

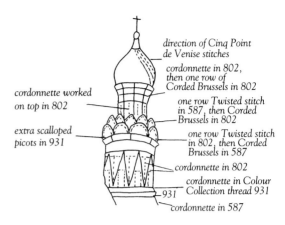

direction of Cinq Point de Venise stitches

cordonnette in 802, then one row of Corded Brussels in 802

cordonnette worked on top in 802

one row Twisted stitch in 587, then Corded Brussels in 802

extra scalloped picots in 931

one row Twisted stitch in 802, then Corded Brussels in 587

cordonnette in 802

cordonnette in Colour Collection thread 931

931

cordonnette in 587

9d   tower C

side of the work, and work a row of Cinq Point de Venise before fastening off. Repeat these two rows until the area is filled. *Do not work the row of single stitches to take the thread back to the left-hand side as you would normally do in the Cinq Point de Venise stitch.* The cordonnette is in no. 931.

The first section under the dome is worked in one strand of gold thread and corded Brussels with the cordonnette in the same colour. The next two bands are worked in no. 587 and Corded Brussels, apart from the middle cordonnette and one row underneath, which are in no. 802.

The middle section of the tower is in no. 587 and Corded Brussels with extra vertical cordonnettes in no. 802 added on top of the stitches.

The top row of hoops has a Twisted stitch edge in no. 587 and a cordonnette in no. 931. The rest of the hoop is Corded Brussels in no. 802; the small black asterisks are stitched on afterwards. The second row of hoops has a Twisted stitch edge in no. 802 and a cordonnette in no. 931; the rest of the hoop is in no. 587 with small couronnes in no. 802 added afterwards.

The next band is worked in no. 931 and Corded Brussels with a scalloped cordonnette in the same colour. The section beneath is in

Corded Brussels (no. 587) with a cordonnette of the same colour.

The zigzag section is worked in no. 587 and Corded Brussels with the triangular cordonnettes in the same colour; but those worked on top of the stitches are in no. 802.

The bottom sections are worked in Corded Brussels (no. 587) with cordonnettes as shown in diagram 9d.

Stage 4: Tower D

The dome is filled with corded Brussels in no. 898; then rows of Cinq Point de Venise in no. 931 are worked on top in curved lines. The cordonnette is in no. 898.

The tiny section under the dome is worked in Alençon beads (no. 802); the cordonnette is in the same colour. The area directly underneath has a Twisted stitch edging and cordonnette in no. 931. The rest of this section is in Corded Brussels (no. 587). The bottom cordonnette is a scalloped one.

The remainder of the tower is worked in Corded Brussels; the next area down is worked in no. 587 with extra cordonnettes in no. 802. The small area above the hoop section is in no. 802 with cordonnette and small couronnes in the same colour.

The hoop section itself has a green background with hoops of no. 587; these have a no. 802 cordonnette. The green areas have a cordonnette in the same colour, including a scalloped edging at the top of this section.

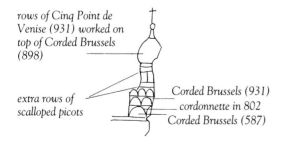

rows of Cinq Point de Venise (931) worked on top of Corded Brussels (898)

extra rows of scalloped picots

Corded Brussels (931)
cordonnette in 802
Corded Brussels (587)

9e tower D

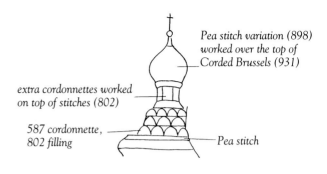

Pea stitch variation (898) worked over the top of Corded Brussels (931)

extra cordonnettes worked on top of stitches (802)

587 cordonnette, 802 filling

Pea stitch

9f tower E

Stage 5: Tower E

The dome has a background of no. 931, then the Pea stitch variation 2 (no. 898) worked over the top; the cordonnette is in the latter colour.

The next area down is in gold thread, as used for the other towers. The following section is in Corded Brussels (no. 587) with extra cordonnettes in no. 802. The area below is again worked in Corded Brussels, beginning with no. 802 and changing halfway down to no. 931; small couronnes may be added afterwards.

The hoop section is all worked in the same way; the background is in no. 931, the hoops are in no. 802 with a no. 587 cordonnette, and the small black asterisks are stitched on afterwards.

The section below the hoop section is in the Colour Collection thread and Pea stitch. The bottom area is in Corded Brussels beginning with no. 931 and changing halfway down to no. 587; the cordonnettes are the colour of the adjacent stitches.

Stage 6: The Main Tower

The small dome at the top and the next four sections are all worked in one strand of the gold thread. Two of the areas have a Twisted stitch edge; these are marked on diagram 9g.

The sloping section of the tower is worked in no. 587 and in Williamson stitch; this stitch is

9 St Basil's Cathedral, designed and worked by the author

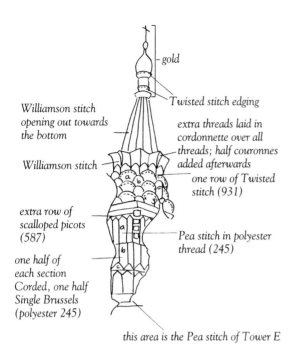

- gold

Williamson stitch opening out towards the bottom

Twisted stitch edging

Williamson stitch

extra threads laid in cordonnette over all threads; half couronnes added afterwards

one row of Twisted stitch (931)

extra row of scalloped picots (587)

Pea stitch in polyester thread (245)

one half of each section Corded, one half Single Brussels (polyester 245)

this area is the Pea stitch of Tower E

9g main tower

9h necklace based on the onion-shaped dome

opened out towards the bottom and closed in to become Corded Brussels at the top. The cordonnettes are in the same colour. The next area down is also worked in Williamson stitch with the same cordonnettes. Half-couronnes have been added to two of the cordonnettes to provide extra interest. The jagged area above the hoop section is in no. 802, Corded Brussels, with cordonnettes the same colour.

The hoop section itself is worked in two ways. The larger hoops have a Twisted stitch edge in no. 931, then two or three rows of no. 802 as the cord and no. 587 as the stitches, finishing with no. 802. The small hoops have one row of no. 587 and the rest is in no. 802. Small black asterisks are stitched onto the larger hoops and a French knot is stitched onto the smaller ones. All the cordonnettes, including

the one at the bottom of this section, are in no. 931.

The two narrow areas below the hoop section are in Corded Brussels, the top one in no. 802 and the second in no. 587. The cordonnettes are in the same colour with scallops added to the lower one.

Areas **a**, **b** and **c** are worked in the Colour Collection thread. The archways in section **a** are in Pea stitch and the background in Corded Brussels. The tiny rectangles are worked in Corded Brussels, using the silk thread no. 802 with a no. 587 cordonnette. The upturned arches in section **b** are worked half in Corded and half in Single Brussels with cordonnettes of the same colour. Section **c** is in Corded Brussels.

The arches in the next section are worked in Corded Brussels (no. 587) with small couronnes added afterwards. The final section is worked in the Colour Collection thread and Corded Brussels with a cordonnette of the same colour.

10

Tower Bridge

MATERIALS NEEDED

Gutermann pure silk 200/3:
 Nos 198. 138, 524 and 179 (fawn)
 736, 701 (grey)
 703 (turquoise)
 000 (black)

STITCHES

Williamson, Ardenza bars and Corded Brussels

INSTRUCTIONS

Stage 1
Lay the cordonnet in the usual way but *do not* lay a cordonnet along the supporting wires at each side, or along the crossed wires that join the towers. These are stitched on afterwards.

Stage 2: The Towers
Begin with the small corner towers, excluding the turrets. Decide from which side the light is coming and shade accordingly, using the three darker fawns. The stitches should be worked lengthways to emphasise the height of the tower. Each flat section of wall is worked lengthways, using the horizontal shading technique, but the small tramline sections that run round the tower have a line of Twisted stitch along the upper edge and are worked horizontally. The turrets are worked in Corded Brussels stitch with large Twisted stitches, in a paler colour, stitched on afterwards (over the top of the existing stitches) to represent the window struts. The sloping roofs of the main towers are worked in Corded Brussels, using the grey threads; a looped picot, in gold, is worked along the

straight edge at the very tops of the towers. The spikes at the top of each turret can be stitched on after the piece has been mounted. The road archway should be fairly dark and is worked in dark grey and black, using the horizontal shading technique.

Stage 3: The Windows
On the flat sides of the tower, the larger windows and the very top windows are worked in Williamson stitch. The smaller windows are worked as open veins. Large Twisted stitches, in a paler colour, are worked on top of the Williamson stitch in the larger windows, to represent the different sections.

Stage 4: The Cordonnette
For the most part this is worked in the same colour as the adjacent stitches, laying down four extra threads. Note that the cordonnette on the corners of the main towers is worked along the complete length and the horizontal sections are worked separately. Small picots may be worked along the top-most edge to add interest.

Stage 5: The Tower Supports
These are worked laying down eight extra threads and working Ardenza bars along them all.

Stage 6: Between the Towers
Sections **a** are worked in Corded Brussels, using darker grey thread. Sections **b** are worked in the same stitch but in the palest fawn; a small red shape or cross may be stitched on afterwards. Sections **c** should be left so that the fawn cross-wires can be stitched on when the work has been mounted.

An ordinary cordonnette is worked along all

10 Tower Bridge, designed and worked by the author

these edges, including those which have been left empty. The cordonnette along the edge of the cross-wires is turquoise and not fawn.

Stage 7: The Bridge

The underside of the bridge will be dark and should therefore be worked in black or dark-grey Corded Brussels. Sections **d**, which have the metal struts in them, can be stitched on afterwards as already described. The 'road' edge should be worked in Corded Brussels, using the palest fawn, with turquoise Twisted stitches on top to represent the railings.

Stage 8: The Supporting Wires

Make a turquoise cord, using three threads, and stitch into place once the work has been mounted. For the vertical supports and the cross-wires, make a cord using two threads and the palest fawn; stitch these into place. Once the work has been mounted, small couronnes and decorative stitches may be added for extra interest.

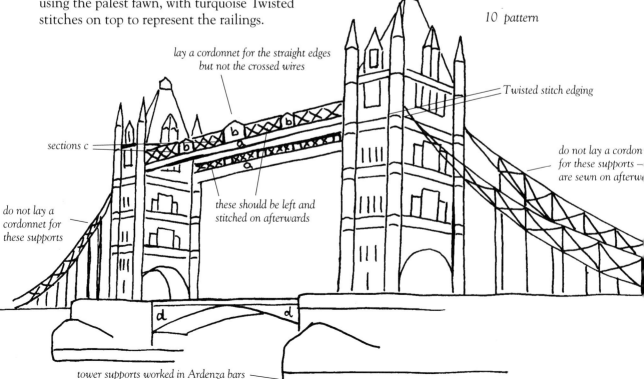

10 pattern

lay a cordonnet for the straight edges but not the crossed wires

Twisted stitch edging

sections c

do not lay a cordon
for these supports —
are sewn on afterwa

do not lay a
cordonnet for
these supports

these should be left and
stitched on afterwards

d

d

tower supports worked in Ardenza bars

11
Powys Castle

11 Powys Castle, designed and worked by Pat Gibson

MATERIALS NEEDED

Gutermann pure silk 200/3 in terracotta
   colours, nos 476 and 81
Pure silk 100/3, nos 582 and 583
Madeira metallic thread, no. 437 FS2/2 no. 20
Mica (obtainable from craft shops)
Felt for padding

STITCHES USED

Corded Brussels, French and Bullion knots

INSTRUCTIONS

Stage 1: The Castle
The castle sections are worked in Corded
Brussels with the chimneys stitched straight
onto the background. Small pieces of mica are
put behind the windows as you sew the pieces
on, and C4 (see diagram 11) has felt padding.

11a yew trees

11 castle sections

Stage 2: The Yew Trees
These are worked in dark-green thread. Tree
Y4 (diagram 11a) has French knots worked on
top of the lace stitches. In section Y5 the yew
trees are worked as one piece.

Stage 3: Terraces
In the photograph these are worked in
machine embroidery, using the same threads as
for the castle, but they could also be worked in
Corded Brussels, adding texture in the form of
French knots. The archways are in the
Madeira thread.

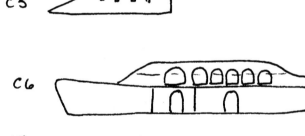

11b terraces

Stage 4: Shrubs
These are all worked onto separate pieces of
painted calico as clusters of French and
Bullion knots. They are then cut out, leaving
spare material round the edge, which is
gathered up, using running stitches, and
padded as the shrubs are sewn into place.
Various threads can be used in different
thicknesses and different colours; some of the
Bullion knots were worked in a green dacron
thread 25 mm. in diameter (used by
fishermen).

11c shrubs

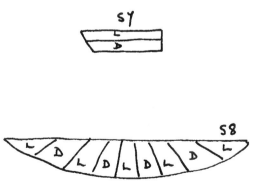

11d staircase

Stage 6: The Lawn

Using the two greens in the 100/3 thread, work in stripes, lengthening the stitches at the outside edge to keep the stripes neat. When changing colours, remember to introduce the new colour as the cord first (in this case for one row only).

Order of Mounting

The pieces of castle and the small bush behind the staircase are stitched on first and the chimneys worked onto the background. The staircase and yew trees come next, then the arched terraces. The bushes S5 are worked straight onto the background, stitching in the small piece of lawn as you work. Finally come the large bushes and, last of all, the lawn.

Key to Diagram 11f			
C 1–4	Castle	S 1–5	Bushes
C 5–6	Terraces	S 7	Top Lawn
C 7	Stairway	S 8	Bottom Lawn
		Y 1–5	Yew Trees

Stage 5: Staircase

This is also worked in Corded Brussels, in the same colour and thread as the castle.

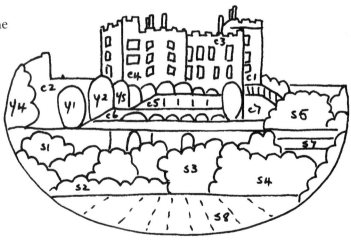

11e top and bottom lawns

11f pattern

———12———
Market Hall

MATERIALS NEEDED

Gutermann pure silk 100/3 and 200/3 (or thread of equivalent thickness):

Nos 221, 838 and 114 (rusts, 200/3)
802 (cream, 200/3)
817 (dark brown, 100/3)
000 (black, 100/3)
545 and 224 (greys, either 100/3 or 200/3)

Perspex

SUGGESTED STITCH

Corded Brussels

INSTRUCTIONS

Stage 1: Tudor Brickwork

You will need to use the 200/3 thread for the brickwork as the sections are tiny. To give the wooden beams a little character, work them in two colours, using the vertical shading. The larger beams and supports may be worked in the thicker thread in corresponding colours.

Stage 2: The Windows

These are leaded and could be worked as large Twisted stitches across the whole window section. The cordonnette would then be worked afterwards. The perspex could be added as you sew the finished building onto its background.

Stage 3: The Roof

This consists of old tiles and needs to have a patchy appearance. You can achieve this effect by using two or three needles with different

12 Market Hall, Singleton

close-up of brick pattern

12 pattern

threads, laying down two or three cords and picking up the different cords as you need them. It will not matter if there are cords loose at the back because the lace will be stitched onto a piece of background material. Once the roof has been filled in, extra straight stitches can be worked to give the effect of tiles. (You

will not need to cover the whole roof in this way – groups of stitches will be enough.)

Stage 4: The Stairs and the Floor
These are stone and should be worked in the greys, using the vertical shading technique and a darker grey to produce the shadows.

13

Medallion

13 pattern

The pattern for this medallion was taken from a circular window.

MATERIALS NEEDED

Dragonfly 140
Gutermann pure silk 100/3

STITCHES USED

Corded Brussels, Pea, Williamson and Twisted

INSTRUCTIONS

Stage 1
Each alternate section is worked in Corded Brussels with a Twisted stitch edge.

ROW 1: Begin at **a** in diagram 13 and work a Twisted stitch row to **b**. Whip the cord back (into each loop) to **a**.

ROW 2: Whip your thread to **c** and work two stitches; hook into the next Twisted stitch loop; take your cord back and hook onto a loop on the other side.

ROW 3: Work a slightly longer row of Corded Brussels.

Continue in this way until the shape is filled, incorporating a Four Pin bud to break up the Corded Brussels.

Stage 2
The remaining shapes round the outside are in Pea stitch with a foundation row (**e** to **f**) lengthening the rows each time.

Stage 3
The narrow circle is worked in Williamson stitch, working round the circle each time.

ROW 1: Begin with a Twisted stitch row along the outside edge, hook into your first stitch and whip back.

13a Medallion 2

13b Medallion 3

13c Medallion 4

13 Medallion, design taken from a circular window and worked by the author

ROW 2: Work the single Brussels row of the Williamson stitch. Each time you complete the circle, hook into the first stitch of that row.

Stage 4
Each petal in the centre has an edge of Twisted stitch and one row of stitches.

ROW 1: Work a row of Twisted stitch in the usual way, whipping the cord back.

ROW 2: Work a row of ordinary stitches (Single Brussels) and whip a cord back into each loop before fastening off; this strengthens the outside edge.

Stage 5
Lay down extra threads round the centre circle so that a couronne may be worked after the cordonnette has been completed.

Stage 6
First work the cordonnette for the outside shapes, followed by that for the larger circle. The cordonnette for the smaller circle is worked after the one for the petals, so that you can just catch the top of the petal in passing. Work the couronne last of all.

14

Conservatory (Syon Park)

14 *The Conservatory at Syon Park, designed and worked by Molly Buckle*

14 pattern **Enlarge by 200%**

14a bushes

MATERIALS NEEDED

Gutermann pure silk 100/3:
   Nos 179 and 524 (browns)
   96 (ecru)
   152 and 271 (greens, for the bushes)

STITCHES USED

Corded and Single Brussels, and Twisted

INSTRUCTIONS

Stage 1: The Top Arch and Main Pillars

The top archway is worked in Corded Brussels, using the darker brown. Single spaces are left and edged with a cordonnette in the same colour. The main pillars have two or three rows of Corded Brussels worked lengthways, which then open out to Single Brussels and close again into Corded Brussels to give a rounded effect.

Stage 2: The Dome

This is worked in Argentan ground, using the ecru colour. It is bordered at the bottom by a narrow section of Corded Brussels, a variety of wheels and another section of Corded Brussels. The two larger circles are also in ecru; these have an edging of Twisted stitch with large Twisted stitches across the circle and a small couronne in the middle.

Stage 3: The Smaller Archway

This is worked in the lighter brown and in Corded Brussels. The pillars are in the same stitch with a vein worked down the middle.

Stage 4: The Bushes

These are worked in Corded and Single Brussels, using the two greens. You could use other stitches such as Pea or Cinq Point de Venise if you wanted to add more texture.

Note the original way of mounting the work. The mount stands away from the work and extra pillars have been painted onto the mount and cut to shape, giving added depth.

15

Metallic Brooch

15 pattern (taken from a window)

MATERIALS NEEDED

Madeira metallic thread no. 40, shade 260
Madeira metallic thread no. 15, Art 9815
 (silver)
Gutermann pure silk 100/3 (black)
Silver beads
Brooch pin

STITCHES USED

Corded Brussels and Treble Twisted

INSTRUCTIONS

Lay the cordonnet in the usual way, using the
three strands of Art 9815 silver thread.

Stage 1
Fill in areas **A** and **B** with Corded Brussels,
making your foundation row from **a** to **b**;

lengthen the row slightly each time so that
you are gradually working round the curve. To
begin with, I used no. 260 thread for cord and
stitches, but towards the inner section of the
curve I changed to no. 260 for the cord and to
silver for the stitches. This helps to give a
shaded effect.

Stage 2
Areas **C** are worked in one strand of the silver
thread and in Treble Twisted stitch. Begin a
foundation row at **c**, lengthening the rows
each time so that you begin to work round the
curve.

Stage 3
Work the cordonnettes along each edge, using
the same thread as for the stitches in that
particular section.

Stage 4
With ordinary sewing thread, sew straight

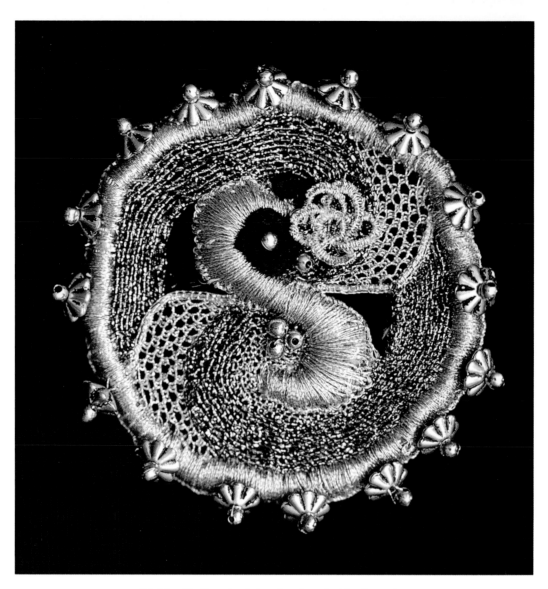

15 Metallic Brooch, designed and worked by the author

stitches across the tramlines of the outside circles at ½ cm. intervals. Thread a thicker thread under these stitches until there is a firm ridge of threads round the outside of the brooch. Lay on four extra silver threads (three strands each time) and buttonhole over all of them to create a raised edge.

N.B. You will need to work the buttonhole stitches very closely together and make sure that they lie parallel to each other.

Stage 5
Sew straight stitches across the centre section in the same way as for the edge. Thread a thicker thread under these stitches, leaving out those at the end as they become full. In this way you should create a tapered effect at each end. Again lay on extra threads and buttonhole over them all. When you reach the centre point **d**, pull your thread up slightly each time so the edge of the button-hole stitch is eventually on the opposite side.

Stage 6
Make small couronnes and flowers to sew onto the brooch after you have taken it off its backing; beads may be added at this stage as well.

16

Brass Door Knocker

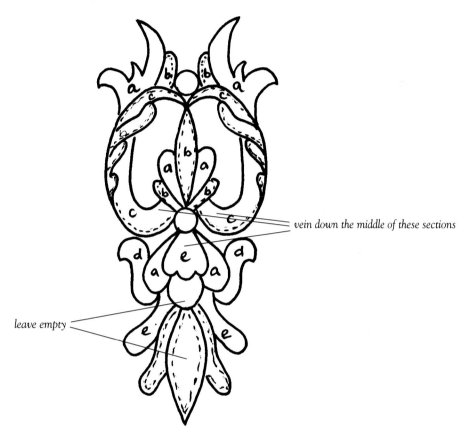

vein down the middle of these sections

leave empty

16 pattern (designed by the author)

MATERIALS NEEDED

Gutermann pure silk 100/3, no. 58
Madeira 15, no. 22 (gold)

STITCHES USED

Corded Brussels, Pea, Twisted and Spider's Web

INSTRUCTIONS

Sections **a** are worked in a very close Pea stitch the length of the shape.

Sections **b** are worked in gold Corded Brussels with a Twisted stitch edging.

Sections **c** are Corded Brussels with a Twisted stitch edging worked in the silk thread.

Sections **d** are Corded Brussels in the silk thread.

Sections **e** are Corded Brussels in gold thread.

The bottom three sections are worked with Twisted stitch edging and two rows of Corded Brussels. The last row is strengthened by hooking the cord into each loop back to the beginning of the row. The two small circles are worked as Spider's Webs, the top one in silk and the centre one in gold.

17
Stained-Glass Window

17 pattern (taken from a door at Tobacco Dock, London)

MATERIALS NEEDED

Gutermann pure silk 100/3:
Nos 383 for the flower and sections **e**
283 and 585 for the leaves

SUGGESTED STITCHES

Pea, Williamson, Corded Brussels,
Treble variation 2, Spider's Web, Twisted and
Four Pin buds

INSTRUCTIONS

Stage 1: **The Flower**
Work sections **a** in Williamson stitch, following the curve of the petal, and sections **b** in
Treble variation 2. The centre of the flower
may be worked in Corded Brussels and section
c as a Spider's Web.

Stage 2: The Leaves
Sections **d** are worked in a close Pea stitch,
following the curve of the leaves. The small
leaves are worked in Corded Brussels with a
Four Pin bud. The remaining leaves are also in
Corded Brussels but with a Twisted stitch
edging (indicated by the dotted lines). The
buds could be worked in Corded Brussels,
using the same colour as for the flower.

18

Designs from Doorplates

*Design from a doorplate
in Luton Museum*

*This design could be joined
in a circle to make a mat, or
repeated to make an edging
for a tablecloth*

More designs from a doorplates

Out and About

19

European Sampler

The designs on this sampler are all worked as separate pieces of needlelace and then sewn onto a net background. The photographs show a drawing of the finished sampler and of the pieces already worked, using mainly Corded Brussels and Pea stitch. The rest of the designs are included as patterns only, and you could work them with your own ideas.

19 pattern

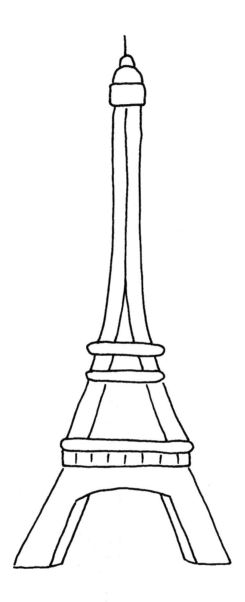

19a pattern

19:1 European Sampler, designed by Iris Wallbank

19:2 Windsor Castle, Great Britain, worked by the author

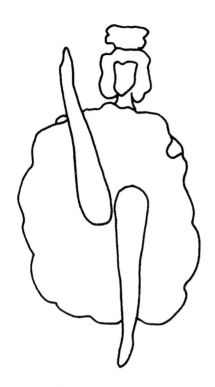

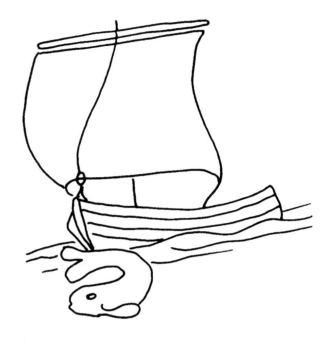

19b cancan girl, France – pattern

19c fishing boat, Portugal – pattern

19d mermaid, Denmark – pattern

19e lacemaker, Belgium – pattern

the flowers could be embroidered onto the net afterwards

19f windmill, Holland – pattern

19:3 The Eiffel Tower, France, worked by the author

the waves could be embroidered or tamboured onto the net afterwards

19g the Leaning Tower of Pisa and gondola, Italy – pattern

19i the children with the Pied Piper, Germany – pattern

19h the Pied Piper of Hamlin, Germany – pattern

19j the Little People, Ireland – pattern

19k Matador, Spain – pattern

19l border, top-left corner

19m the Bridge, Luxembourg – pattern

19n the Acropolis, Greece – pattern

19o border, bottom-right corner

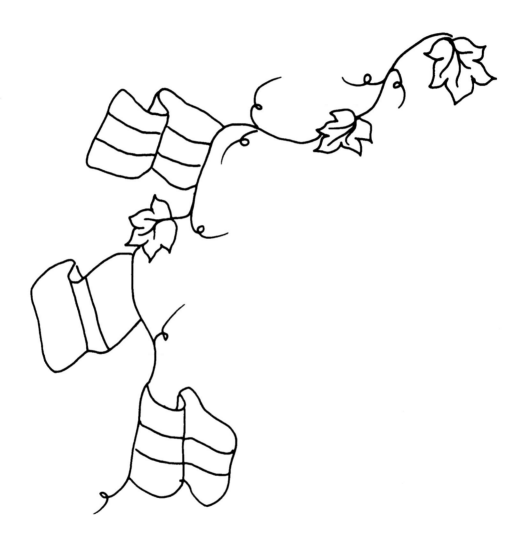

19p Ireland, Spain and Luxembourg – flags

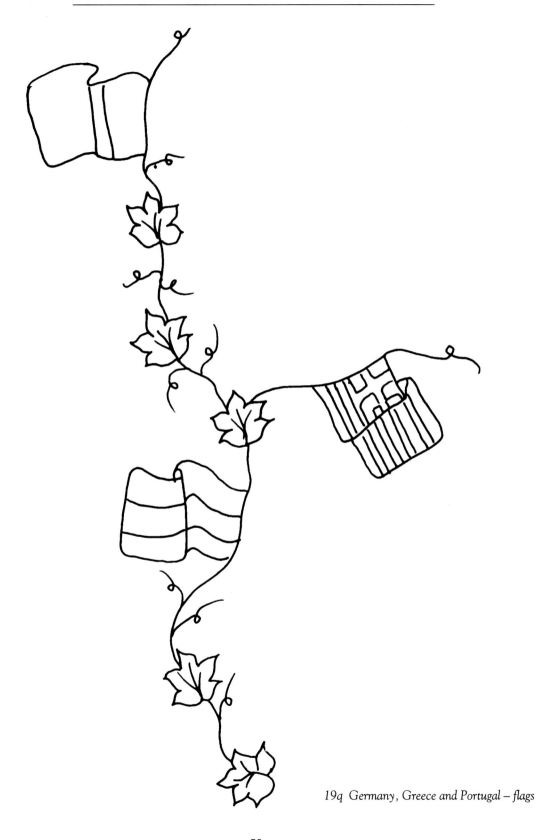

19q Germany, Greece and Portugal – flags

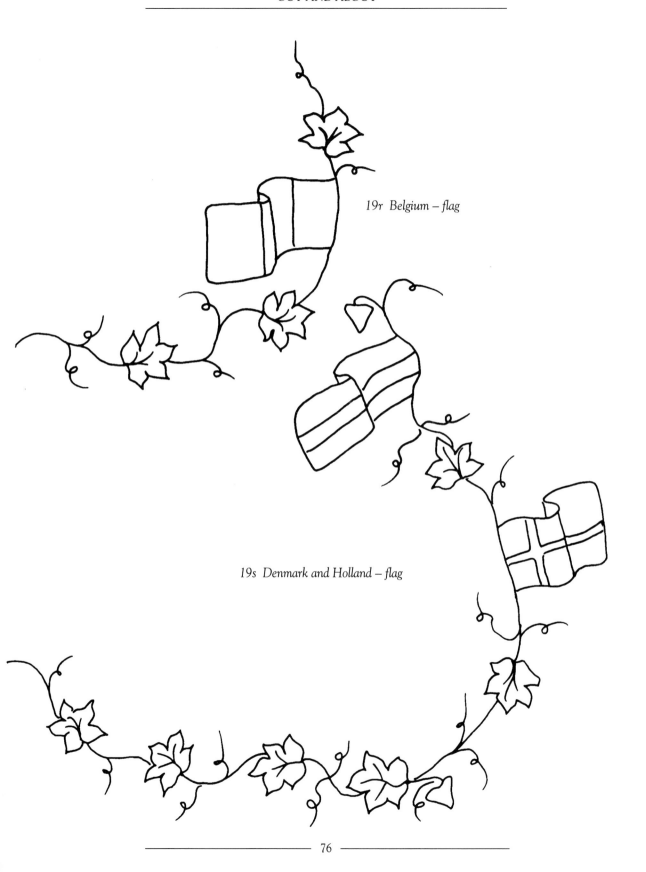

19r Belgium – flag

19s Denmark and Holland – flag

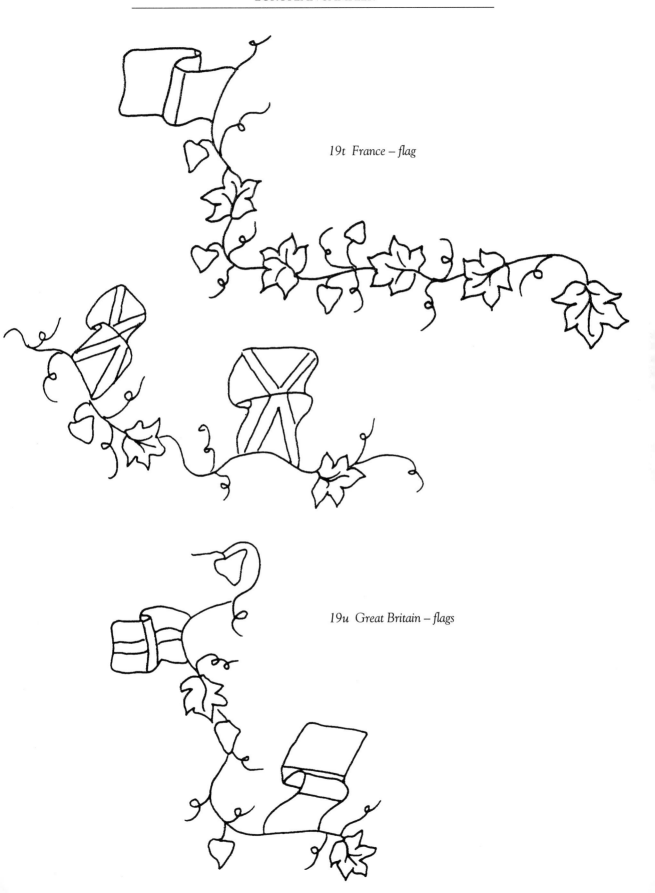

19t France – flag

19u Great Britain – flags

20

St James's Park

20 St James's Park, designed and worked by the author

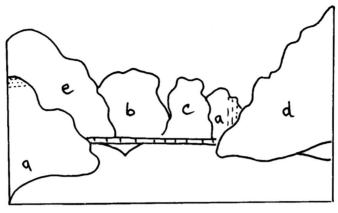

20 pattern

MATERIALS NEEDED

Gutermann Colour Collection, polyester threads (Forest greens and Heron greys)

STITCHES USED

Pea, Cinq Point de Venise, Treble Brussels, Corded Brussels with open shading, Water stitch and Treble variation 1

INSTRUCTIONS

Stage 1: The Trees

Having laid the cordonnet, work sections **a** in Pea stitch, using a medium green and following the direction of stitches as indicated. Section **b** is worked using Treble Brussels and a darker thread. Section **c** is Treble variation 1, again using a darker shade of green. The large tree in the foreground (**d**) is worked in a bright green, using Corded Brussels and incorporating open shaded areas. Section **e** is in Cinq Point de Venise, using a mid-green.

Stage 2: The Water

This is worked in Water stitch; work a medium-grey filling first in the two areas on each side of the bridge support.

Stage 3: The Bridge

The tiny support is filled with Corded Brussels in a darker grey; a row of Twisted stitch is worked next to represent the railings. The small piece of footpath on the right is worked in Corded Brussels and a lighter grey.

Stage 4: The Cordonnette

Using the same colour thread as for the filling stitches and laying down four extra threads, work each cordonnette separately, starting with the tree that is furthest back. Work the cordonnette for the bridge before those for the two foremost trees. The cordonnette round the three outside edges should be worked last of all. A small red French knot has been added to the bridge to represent the bright coat of someone crossing it.

21 Dolphin and Girl, designed and worked by the author

21

Dolphin and Girl

MATERIALS NEEDED

Dragonfly thread 140
Gutermann pure silk 100/3 (white)

STITCHES USED

Corded Brussels

INSTRUCTIONS

Stage 1

Prepare a tracing and draw in the shaded areas; this will help when working the stitches. Use this pattern underneath the draughtsman's linen so that you can see the marked area. Note that the darker areas are where the stitches are opened out to let the background colour show through. Lay the cordonnet using a double silk thread.

Stage 2

ROW 1: Begin your first row of Corded Brussels at **a** and work to **b**. When taking the cord back, hook it into alternate stitches over the shaded section, then proceed in the usual way to the end of the row.

ROW 2: Work this row in close corded Brussels up to the shaded area, then work into alternate stitches, thus opening out the stitching; the cord should not show because it has been hooked into the loops of the previous row. Continue in this way, using the shaded areas to guide you and lengthening the rows to keep the curve of the body. The girl's body is worked in the same way.

Stage 3

Work the cordonnette in the usual way, laying in four extra threads of Dragonfly 140. If you want to mount the finished lace in a free-standing position, fine wire should be added to the cordonnette, instead of adding two of the threads.

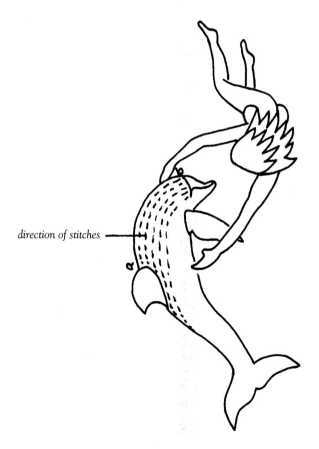

direction of stitches

21 pattern

22 Waste Ground, designed and worked by the author

22

Waste Ground

MATERIALS NEEDED

Gutermann pure silk 100/3:

GRASSES: nos 271 (green) and 186 (fawn)

RAGWORT: nos 104 and 412 (yellows)

MALLOW: nos 211 and 321 (pinks); 283 and 839 (greens); 391, 810 and 183 (purples) for the dead flower

Small amount of wadding for stuffing

COW PARSLEY: nos 800 (white) and 271 (green)

ROSE HIPS: nos 364 (red), 350 (orange), 000 (black) and 271 (green)

Oval bead (red or orange)

POPPY: nos 26 (red) and 000 (black)

Black stamens

A domed button with shank

DAISY: no. 800 (white) and yellow

You will also need fine florist's wire, fine green covered wire and florist's gutta (green tape to bind stems).

BEDSTEAD: DMC Fil or Clair (gold thread)

Small brass-coloured beads

POST: nos 439 (brown) and 000 (black)

Fine brown covered wire

Felt

You will also need a selection of greens for the French knots and padding for the tiny clumps of knots at the base of the bedstead.

STITCHES AND TECHNIQUES USED

Corded Brussels, Venetian Picots, vertical shading and Spider's Web

INSTRUCTIONS

Grasses

1 Lay the cordonnet in the usual way. Using

22 grass

two needles and working both from the same side, lay the fawn thread down as a cord. Work the stitches using the green thread, hooking a loop of fawn thread through occasionally. When you hook this through, carry on working the stitches in the usual way – you do not need to anchor the loop. It is easier to loop the cord if it has been taken back in the same direction as the stitches, so you may need to take the cord back from right to left and then back again from left to right. (It does not matter if you have more than one cord at the back because these will be inside the grass.) Fill the shape and take off the backing. *Do not work a cordonnette.*

2 Run gathering stitches along the top of the shape and gather up. Stuff the shape with wadding or paper tissue and insert a piece of green covered wire with a small loop at the top (this stops the wire from pulling out). Sew up the sides of the shape and fasten at the bottom. Make three of these shapes.

Ragwort

1 Make a small yellow couronne with Venetian picots round the edge (see couronne 9, p. 118). Work a small circle of Corded Brussels in darker yellow, slightly larger than the centre of the couronne. *Do not work a cordonnette.*

2 Make small gathering stitches round the circle, gather up and pad out with paper tissue or wadding; add a piece of green covered wire at the same time.

3 Stitch this small padded ball to the couronne, allowing the wire to hang through the middle. Make a number of such balls and twist the wires together to form a complete flower. Each flower is on its own wire but joins the main stem 4 cm. from the flower head.

Mallow

1: THE MAIN FLOWER Work five petals in Corded Brussels, using the vertical-shading technique. When working the cordonnette, lay down wire instead of extra threads; work the stitches close together so that the wire does not show through. Leave extra wire when you begin and end the cordonnette. Twist these ends together; this will give you something to hold onto when putting the flower together.

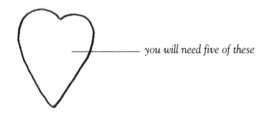

you will need five of these

22a mallow: petal for flower

2 Make a centre as you would make a grass but using pink with grey loops. The wire which is added must be a long piece as this will be the main stem.

3 The sepals are worked as one piece and stitched under the flower.

22b mallow: sepal for main flower

22c mallow: petals for dead flower

4: THE DEAD FLOWER To make the dead mallow flower, work the three long petals, using the vertical-shading technique with the darker purple at the top of the petal. Wire the cordonnette and add a piece of green covered wire when you fix the petals together. Twist the petals so that they look as if they are shrivelled up. Make some sepals to stitch on at the bottom of this flower.

5: THE BUDS The buds are made in three sections. Work the larger sepal shape in Corded Brussels with a Twisted stitch edging; wire the cordonnette. Work the smaller sepal shape in Corded Brussels, with an extra cordonnette running from each point to the middle of each sepal. This gives an extra ridge when the sepal is bent a little round the pink bud. Work two tiny pink petals. Work an ordinary cordonnette, bend a piece of green covered wire into a loop at the top, and put this in between the petals. Add padding and sew up the sides of the petals. Thread the wire through the smaller sepals first and sew into place under the pink bud. Repeat this with the larger sepals, making sure that they are arranged so that the smaller and larger sepals alternate.

6: TO MAKE UP Hold two petals of the main flower together and wind a separate piece of wire round immediately under the petals. Add the centre and wire it to the petals, then add the other petals and wire those; pull this wire really tight. Using florist's gutta, begin to gutta the wire, adding the dead flower a little way down. Add the buds further down still.

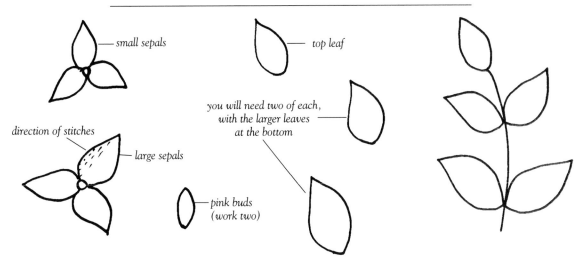

small sepals

top leaf

you will need two of each,
with the larger leaves
at the bottom

direction of stitches

large sepals

pink buds
(work two)

22d mallow: bud and sepals for bud   22e rosehip: leaves   22f rosehip: arrangement of leaves

Cow Parsley

Make a tiny couronne but lay in a piece of wire round half of the couronne so that the ends of the wire are sticking out at each side (see diagram, p. 118). Work the small flower in the usual way. Take the flower off the backing and twist the two pieces of wire together; tie a short length of green thread under the flower, knot and cut off so that the two ends are showing. Make a number of these flowers and twist the wires together to form a head. Gutta the wires further down the stem.

Rosehips

1 Begin with the small black pip at the top of the rosehip. This is a tiny couronne with Venetian picots. Take a piece of fine wire, bend it in half and knot a piece of black cotton or silk three or four times at the bend of the wire. Remove the couronne from its backing and thread the wire through so that the small bunch of knots sits in the centre. Thread the wire through the oval bead. This will be the main stem.

2 Use red or orange thread and wind it round the top of the bead just under the couronne. Work stitches over these threads. Continue to work round and round the bead towards the bottom. When you reach the widest part of the bead it will begin to show through, so it is important to use a bead that is the right

colour. At the bottom of the bead, catch all the stitches together and secure round the wire. Make three rosehips in this way; you can vary them by using a red bead with orange thread and an orange bead with red thread.

3 **The leaves** are worked in Corded Brussels, using two greens and the vertical-shading technique; a centre cordonnette may be worked on top of the stitches. Gutta the stems together, adding the leaves at intervals.

Poppy

1: THE PETALS Lay the cordonnet and draw in the shading lines. (These are just to give you a rough idea, not to be adhered to rigidly.) Lay your needle along the shading line nearest to the edge where you want to begin. Move the needle to the edge, keeping it parallel with the line of shading; this will tell you at which angle to begin your foundation row.

2 Work each petal using the vertical-shading technique. Remember that short rows may be needed in order to change the direction of the rows; by the time you reach the centre of the petal you should be working straight. Work the cordonnette, laying in wire instead of extra threads. Leave extra wire when you begin and at the end of the cordonnette; twist these together.

3: THE CENTRE This is a domed button with a

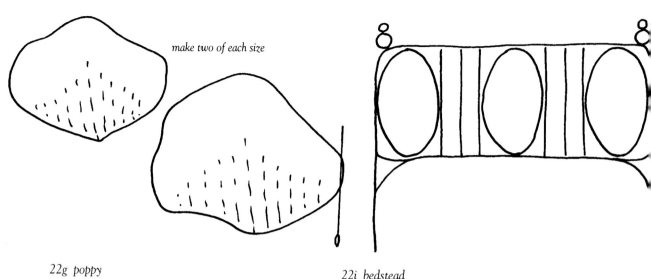

make two of each size

22g poppy

22i bedstead

shank. Work a circle of black Corded Brussels with a larger diameter than that of the button. *Do not work a cordonnette.* Lace this circle over the button so that it is completely covered. thread a piece of wire through the shank and twist to give you something to hold on to. Next work a Spider's Web in green, over the top of the black Corded Brussels, just filling the centre section and not working right to the outside edge.

4: TO MAKE UP Hold together the two small petals and the centre; twist a piece of wire round these very tightly, then add the remaining petals and wind the wire round again. Cut off some of the extra wires and then gutta the remaining stem.

The Daisies
These are worked in two sections and then stitched together. Each petal is worked in Corded Brussels. The centre of each daisy is a tiny couronne.

22h daisy

The Bedstead
This is simply a cordonnette worked in gold thread with wire added so that you can bend it out of shape.

The Post
Stitch a piece of felt onto the background material where the post is going to be, then work a piece of needlelace slightly larger. *Do not work a cordonnette.* Stitch into place over the felt.

Stones and Grass
Stones may be made by working small pieces of needlelace over pieces of card. The tufts of grass are French knots worked on a separate piece of calico then cut out, leaving an extra piece of calico round the edge; turn this in and stitch to the background. Various other things may be added to your picture, such as pieces of wire twisted round the post, or an old wheel frame, again made from wire. Tiny ivy leaves can be made to twist round these wires by winding thread under five radiating stitches (as for the small couronne flowers), then working the stitches inside the circle of threads rather than outside as normal. The knobs on the bedstead are brass beads, sewn on afterwards.

23
Thistle

23 Thistle, designed and worked by Barbara Netherwood

This could be added to the flowers on the *Waste Ground* picture.

MATERIALS NEEDED

Gutermann pure silk thread:
    Nos 585 and 271 (greens)
    211 and 321 for the thistle top

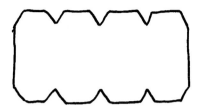

23 pattern

STITCHES USED

Corded Brussels and Venetian Picots

INSTRUCTIONS

Stage 1: The Thistle Body

Work this in Corded Brussels, beginning with the lighter green and working each shaped section first so that they are filled in before taking a cord straight across for a full row. Using the horizontal-shading technique, bring in the darker green and complete the shape.

Stitch in approximately four lines of running stitches (going through all layers of material) on top of the Corded Brussels, *making sure that the stitches alternate on each row*. (These are for your Venetian picots.) Work the Venetian picots by running your working thread under the Corded Brussels until you are at a point to make a picot.

Stage 2: The Head

Stitch the top of the body shape together so that you have a slight dome and pad this with wadding or tissue, incorporating a piece of wire at the same time. Stitch the bottom of the thistle together round the wire.

Knot pieces of the pink thread to the top of the thistle and tease each one out with a needle. When the area is full, cut them to the required length.

The London Bus

MATERIALS NEEDED

DMC Coton Perlé:
    no. 321 (red)
    399 and 400 (grey)
    black
    white
Double-sided iron-on Vilene (small amount)

STITCHES USED

Corded Brussels

INSTRUCTIONS

Stage 1: Windows and Wheels

The windows are worked in mid-grey. The advertisement strip and wheels are worked in dark grey with a centre section of white in the former. The small number section is in black. The wheels are worked from the outside edge to the centre, leaving a hole in the middle and four or five small holes at intervals a little further out.

Stage 2: The Main Body of the Bus

Apart from the white strip that goes across the bus and under the advertisement, the rest of the bus is worked in red. Begin at the top from **a** to **b** and work in horizontal rows right down to the bottom; do not worry too much about the tiny sections in between the windows because the two cordonnettes will meet there.

The symbol on the bottom part of the bus is a small white couronne, sewn on afterwards, with a horizontal cordonnette worked across the middle.

Stage 3: The Platform

The inside of the bus (**c**) is worked in colour 400 lengthways, whilst the stairs are worked horizontally, using 399 and 400 to create the light and dark effect. The handles are cordonnettes worked on top afterwards; these could be embroidered on.

Stage 4: The Advertising Panel

This has 'OXO' embroidered in red on the white background. The other letters are cut from felt backed with double-sided Vilene; they are stuck on afterwards. The number and destination of the bus are embroidered in the small black section.

Stage 5: The Cordonnette

This is worked in the usual way, laying on two extra threads and working stitches over these and the cordonnet. The colour used is that of the adjacent stitches. A black line is embroidered along the top of the upstairs windows, and black straight stitches are worked on the floor of the boarding platform.

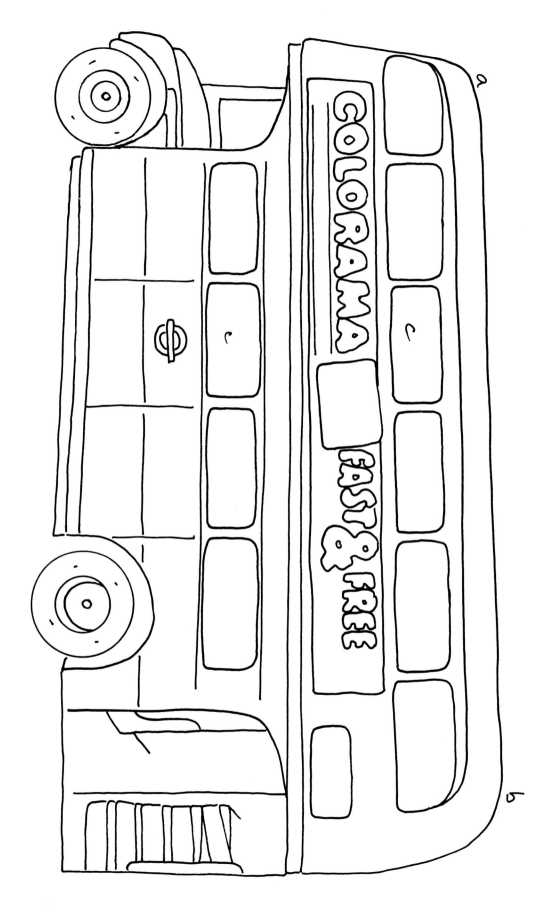

25

Traffic-Light Earrings

25 Traffic-Light Earrings, designed and worked by Barbara Netherwood

MATERIALS NEEDED

Gutermann pure silk, nos 365, 350, 396 and
  black
Earring fittings
Fine chain
Wire

STITCHES USED

Pea and Corded Brussels

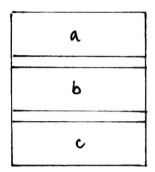

25 pattern

INSTRUCTIONS

Lay a cordonnet in black. Using Pea stitch, fill
in section **a** in red, section **b** in orange and
section **c** in green. The narrow sections in
between are either filled with black Corded
Brussels or made into a padded cordonnette.
When working the outside edge cordonnette,
lay in some fine wire.

Attach a fine chain to the lace, allowing some
of the chain to hang at the bottom, then bend
the lace into a cylindrical shape.

The earrings on the right of the photograph
are worked in the same way but the areas of
black Corded Brussels are larger.

26

Fish from a London Streetlamp

MATERIALS NEEDED

Madeira no. 15 metallic thread or Japanese silk (as supplied by The Carey Company)

STITCHES USED

Williamson, Twisted, Corded and Single Brussels

INSTRUCTIONS

Stage 1: The Body

Lay the cordonnet in the usual way. Work a foundation row from **a** to **b**, then work in Williamson stitch, lengthening the rows until you are working round the curve of the body. Change to Corded Brussels as you work into the tip of the tail, and fill in the other part of the tail in Corded Brussels as well.

Stage 2: The Fins

Fins **c** are worked in Corded Brussels. Fins **d** are worked with the top half in Corded Brussels and the bottom half in Single Brussels.

Stage 3: The Head

Work a row of Twisted stitch from **e** to **f**, then work rows of Corded Brussels backwards and forwards round the head. Section **g** is in Corded Brussels and section **h** in Single Brussels.

Stage 4: The Cordonnette

Most of the cordonnette is worked in the usual way by laying two or four extra threads down, but the areas marked with a thicker line are padded with lots of extra threads.

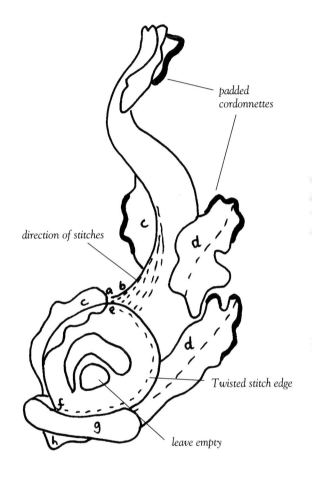

padded cordonnettes

direction of stitches

Twisted stitch edge

leave empty

26 pattern

Stage 5: The Eye

Work a circle of black Corded Brussels, making sure it is larger in diameter than the button. *Do not work a cordonnette.* Lace this circle over the button, then work a Spider's Web on top, in the gold thread used for the fish. Stitch the button in place when the fish has been taken off its backing.

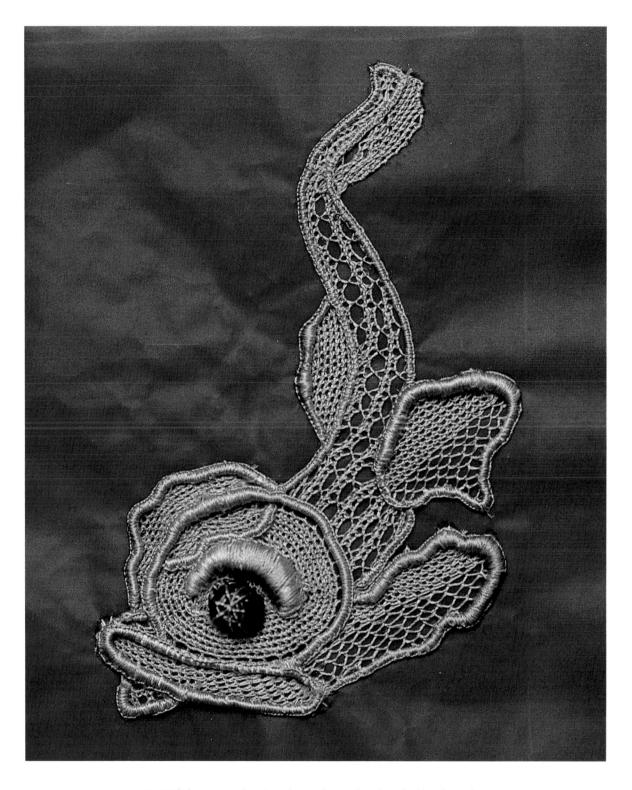

26 Fish from a London Streetlamp, designed and worked by the author

Fish Necklace

27 pattern

The fish shape worked in the previous pattern is ideal for a necklace or brooch. The necklace will need two fishes with highly raised cordon-nettes to help make it chunky and a large domed button for the centre. The button must be covered with Corded Brussels, so you should work a circle large enough to cover the button when the finished piece is laced at the back. *Remember not to work a cordonnette round the circle.*

Having laced the Corded Brussels over the top, you can then work a Spider's Web over the covered button, using either the same thread as for the fish or a co-ordinating thread. After the fish and button have been stitched together, leather thonging can be attached to the fish on each side and necklace fastenings put on the ends.

Stitches and Techniques

Single Brussels

Single Brussels

The Single Brussels stitch is similar to a simple buttonhole or blanket stitch. Having fastened your thread to the cordonnet on the left side of the area to be filled, lay a loop of the working thread from left to right, then take the needle under the cordonnet from the back, with the needle pointing towards you. Bring the needle through the loop you have just made and pull the thread until you can see the loop of the stitch. *Do not leave the stitches too loose or they will move out of place easily; if you make them too tight you will lose the beauty of the stitches.*

ROW 1: Work a row of these stitches along the cordonnet. When you have reached the other side of the area being filled, take the thread under and over the cordonnet ready to begin the next row.

ROW 2: This time the loop of thread is laid from right to left but the rest of the stitch is exactly the same.

Corded Brussels

Corded Brussels

Work a foundation row of buttonhole stitches fairly close together. When you have reached

the cordonnet on the other side, take your working thread under and over this cordonnet and back to the other side of the space being filled. Again take the thread under the cordonnet and hold with the thumb of the left hand until the first stitch of the next row has been worked; this keeps the cord taut.

ROW 1: The next row is worked in buttonhole stitch, but taking in the cord as well as the loop from the previous row.

Double Corded Brussels

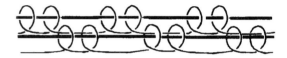

Double Corded Brussels

This stitch is worked in exactly the same way as Corded Brussels but two stitches are worked into each large loop of the previous row. Remember to take the cord across each time before beginning the next row.

Pea Stitch

Work a foundation row, taking the thread under and over the cordonnet on the right-hand side.

ROW 1: Work this row by making a stitch into each of the first two loops from the previous row. Miss two loops, then make a stitch into each of the next two; repeat this to the end of the row.

It is important to work the pattern for as long as possible, even if you work only one or two stitches of a group. If you do not put these part-patterns in, the finished lace will have large holes at the edge of the design.

ROW 2: This row is worked from left to right,

Pea stitch, row 1

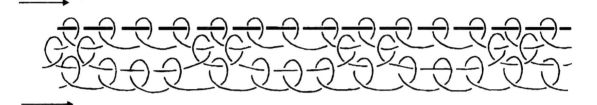

Pea stitch, row 2

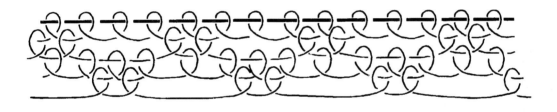

Pea stitch, row 3

working three stitches into the large loop created on the second row and one stitch into the small loop. Repeat to the end of the row.

ROW 3: This row is a repeat of row 1: three stitches = two loops. Work a stitch into each of the two loops made by each group of three stitches.

ROW 4: Repeat row 2.

Pea Stitch Variation 1

ROW 1: Begin with a row of Single Brussels, leaving a space between each stitch large enough for two other stitches.

Pea stitch variation 1

ROW 2: Work this row from right to left, putting two stitches into each loop.

ROW 3: Repeat row 1, putting the single stitches under those of the first row.

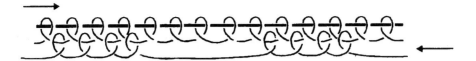

Pea stitch variation 2, row 1

Pea Stitch Variation 2 (with Picots)

Work a foundation row from left to right.

ROW 1: Working back from right to left, work a stitch into the next four loops; leave four loops (five stitches). Repeat to the end of the row.

ROW 2: Work one stitch into the first loop of the group of four stitches in the previous row, then work a picot into the next loop and a stitch into the last loop in this group. Work five stitches into the large loop. Repeat to the end.

ROW 3: Work four stitches into the four loops created by the stitch group from the previous row; repeat to the end.

ROW 4: Repeat row 2.

These rows form the pattern.

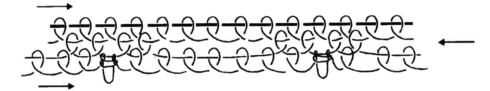

Pea stitch variation 2, row 2

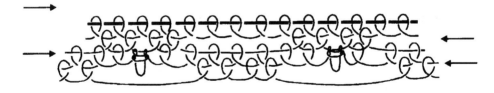

Pea stitch variation 2, row 3

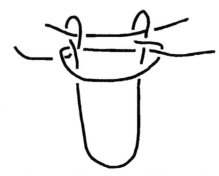

Pea stitch variation 2, an enlarged drawing of a picot

Treble Variation 1

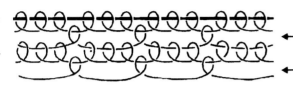

Treble variation 1

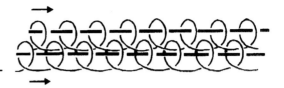

Williamson stitch, row 2

ROW 1: Work three stitches and leave a space; continue to the end of the row.

ROW 2: Work back, putting one stitch into each space left in the previous row.

ROW 3: Work three stitches into each large loop from the previous row, spacing these out so that they resemble the first row.

ROW 4: Repeat the second row.

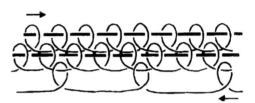

Williamson stitch, row 3

Treble Variation 2

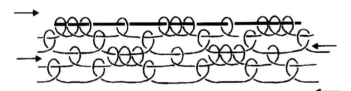

Treble variation 2

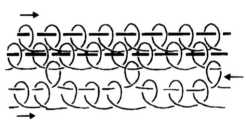

Williamson stitch, row 4

ROW 1: Work three stitches together. Leave a space, work one stitch, leave a space; repeat to the end of the row.

ROW 2: Work back from right to left, putting a single stitch into the loop on each side of the single stitch in the previous row.

ROW 3: Work a single stitch under the group of three in row 1, and three stitches under the single stitch of row 1.

ROW 4: Repeat row 2.

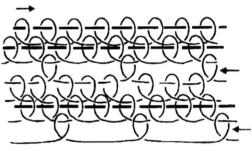

Williamson stitch: a repeat of the pattern

Williamson

ROW 1: Work a row of Single Brussels.

ROW 2: Take a cord back, then work a row of Corded Brussels.

ROW 3: Work this row in Single Brussels but miss out two loops in between each stitch.

ROW 4: Work a row of Single Brussels, replacing the stitches you missed out in the previous row (i.e. making three stitches into

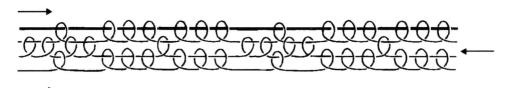

Water stitch

each large loop). Space these stitches out so that they look like an ordinary row of Single Brussels.

Repeat from row 2.

Water Stitch

ROW 1: Work three stitches, leave a space large enough for one stitch; work three more stitches, leave a space large enough for two stitches; work one stitch, leave a space the same as the last one. Repeat to the end of the row.

ROW 2: Working from right to left, work one stitch into the space between each group of three stitches, and two stitches on each side of the single stitch.

ROW 3: Work one stitch between each group of two stitches, and three stitches on each side of the single stitch.

Repeat these rows to fill the space. If you vary the spacing of these groups, even in the same row, you will achieve an uneven effect that resembles ripples on water.

Cinq Point de Venise (Shell Stitch)

ROW 1: Make a buttonhole stitch approximately 4 mm. from the left-hand edge. (If you want the stitches closer, make this space smaller.) Pull the thread up to tension the stitch, then lay the thread round in a loop to the left and make one stitch into the large loop created by the 4 mm. space. When making this stitch, pull the thread up and to the left (this will maintain the tension so that

you do not develop a large slack loop). Now work five stitches over both of these threads, back up towards the original stitch. Make another stitch over the cordonnet, again leaving a 4 mm. space . Repeat the process. Note that the spacing is entirely up to you – 4 mm. is a suggestion only.

ROW 2: Working from right to left, make a Single Brussels stitch into each of the previous loops at the left end of the shell

These two rows form the pattern.

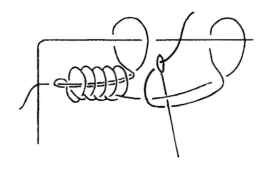

Cinq Point de Venise (Shell stitch)

Twisted Stitch

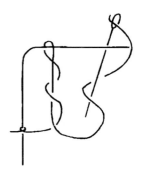

Twisted stitch

This can be used as a foundation row to give an open edge to a design, or to open out veins.

Join your thread to the cordonnet and insert the needle as though you are going to make a stitch. Before you pull the needle through, pick up the thread and take it under and over the needle, moving to the left. Pull the needle through the loop as usual.

Shell Stitch Variation

This stitch looks effective when worked in two colours but can easily be worked in one. However, the following instructions are for two colours.

ROW 1: Work a foundation row, then take a cord back.

ROW 2: This is a row of Corded Brussels. At the end of the row, hook this needle out of the way; *do not take a cord back*.

ROW 3: Join in your second colour at the left-hand side of the work. Now complete a row of Shell stitch (Cinq Point de Venise), missing out a loop between each stitch.

ROW 4: Hook this needle out of the way and take your original thread back, working one stitch at the end of each shell, just as you would for a normal Shell stitch.

ROW 5: Still with your original thread, work two stitches into each loop created in the previous row; take a cord back.

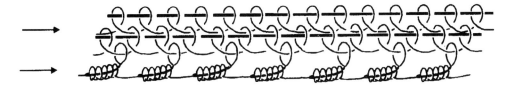

Shell stitch variation, rows 1, 2 and 3

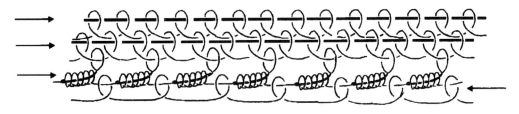

Shell stitch variation, rows 1, 2, 3 and 4

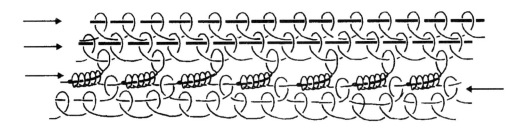

Shell stitch variation, rows 1, 2, 3, 4 and 5

ROW 6: Repeat row 2. Continue in this way. If you want to use the same colour all the time, take the cord back at the end of row 2 by whipping it into each loop.

ROW 7: Take up the second colour and work a row of Shell stitch from right to left.

Twisted Treble

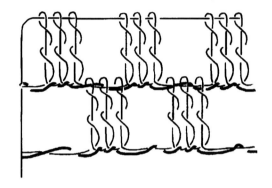

Twisted Treble

ROW 1: Work three Twisted stitches, then leave a space large enough for three more stitches; repeat to the end of the row.

ROW 2: Take a cord back, hooking into each large loop and into each of the smaller ones between the actual stitches.

ROW 3: Repeat row 1, working the three stitches into the large loop each time.

ROW 4: Repeat the second row.

Ardenza Bars

Lay down the extra threads that you would

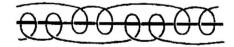

Ardenza bars

normally use for the cordonnette and work two stitches together. Leave a space enough to fit in two more stitches; repeat to the end of the cordonette.

Turn the work round and work back along the cordonnette, putting two stitches into the spaces left when working along the other side. Be careful not to catch in the loop from that previous working.

This stitch adds interest to an otherwise plain cordonnette and also helps the cordonnette to stay flat once the lace has been taken off the backing.

Alençon Beads

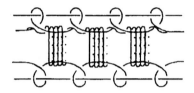

Alençon beads

This stitch is useful for filling a narrow space. Work a Single Brussels stitch along both edges of the shape, making sure that the loops are opposite each other. Wind your working thread into the first loop at the bottom of the space, then loop your thread over the top loop, bringing your needle down the back and up through the bottom loop again. Repeat until you have three or four loops of thread making a kind of lozenge. Wind your thread onto the next set of loops and repeat the process. Do not pull the loops of the lozenge too tight or you will spoil the effect.

Four Pin Bud

This is a diamond pattern created by holes and is normally used to break up a large expanse of Corded Brussels stitch.

STAGE 1: Work Corded Brussels normally

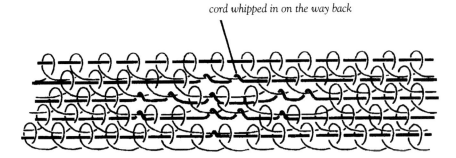

cord whipped in on the way back

until the row *before* you want to begin the bud. Take the cord back, whipping it into the loop or loops which will not be worked on the next row, i.e. in the hole. Work the next row in Corded Brussels, missing the loop or loops where the cord has been whipped in.

STAGE 2: Take the cord back, this time whipping into loops on either side of the large hole left on the previous row and into the large loop. Keep the holes the same size – this means counting carefully. Work the next row of Corded Brussels, leaving out stitches where the cord has been whipped in on the previous row but replacing the stitches which were missed out on the first row of the bud.

STAGE 3: Take the cord back, whipping it into the loops *and* into the stitches between these large loops, i.e. under the first hole. Work a row of Corded Brussels, replacing the stitches left out in the previous row, and missing those stitches which were put back into the first loop. Continue in Corded Brussels.

Argentan Ground

This ground consists of small, buttonholed hexagons. As they need to be evenly spaced, it is easier to work from a pattern. Lay your tracing paper over graph paper and mark out your hexagons, then transfer the tracing to the pattern being worked.

STAGE 1: Use an ordinary sewing cotton to put in the stitches at each corner of the

hexagons; these are bridge stitches and will be removed later.

STAGE 2: Leave a short length of working thread at **a**, take your thread from **a** to **b** (under the bridge stitch) from **b** to **c** to **d** to **e** and to **f**.

STAGE 3: Take the thread back through **e** to **d**, then down to **g** and back again, then through the letters out to **a**, going down to **h** as you did to **g**.

STAGE 4: Take the thread from **a** to **b**, down to **h**, then buttonhole back over the three threads to **b**, through **c** to **d** and down to **g**;

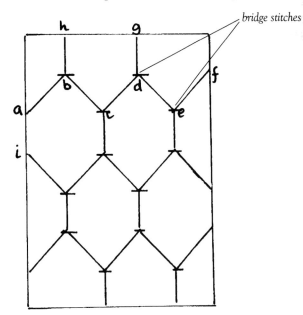

Argentan ground

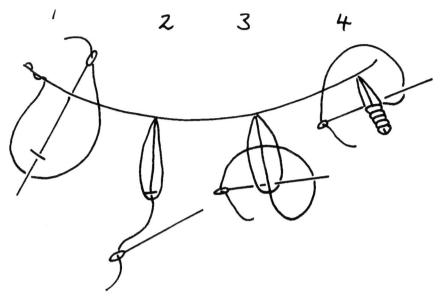

Venetian picots

buttonhole back up to **d** over the three threads. Take the thread through **e** to **f**.

STAGE **5**: Buttonhole back from **f** through **e**, **d**, **c** and **b** to **a**, making sure that you catch the end of the stitches already worked at **d** and **b**.

STAGE **6**: Take the thread along the side of the space from **a** to **i** and begin the process again.

Venetian Picots

Work a line of running stitches parallel to the outline where you need to make the picots. Begin working your cordonnette; when you reach the point for a picot, make a loop of thread as though you were going to make another stitch but take the needle underneath the cordonnet and through the small running stitch as well. This gives you three threads. Turn the work on its side and make a buttonhole stitch over two of these threads at the top near the running stitch (thus fastening the stitches down so that they do not slide off). Work buttonhole stitches down to the cordonnet over all three threads. Carry on with the cordonnette until you reach the spot for the next picot; repeat the process.

To Work a Vein on Top of Existing Stitches

Work the stitches of the cordonnette in the usual way, laying in two or four extra threads. When you need a vein, take half of those threads being laid down, and bring them up to a pin, which is placed where the top of the vein will be. Hook these threads round the pin and take them back to lie with the other threads.

Work the buttonhole stitches of your cordonnette over these threads up to the pin. Take out the pin and put your needle through the small loop that is left. At this point you may be able to pull gently on the threads to ease the loop out of sight.

Take your needle in and out, under the vein already worked, until you are back at the base of the vein. Continue the cordonnette. This is also the way to lay in extra cordonnettes, and is useful if you have small areas of stitching. Stitch over the whole area, then work the cordonnettes on afterwards.

Design showing veins worked on top of stitches

to work a vein on top of stitches

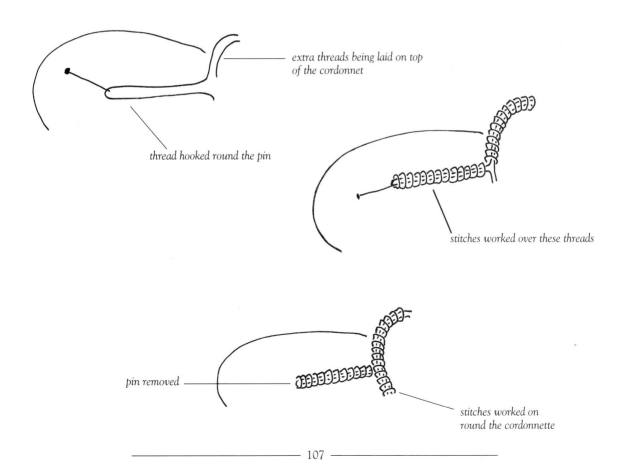

extra threads being laid on top of the cordonnet

thread hooked round the pin

stitches worked over these threads

pin removed

stitches worked on round the cordonnette

Spider's Web

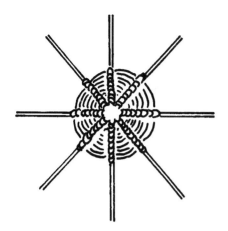

Spider's Web

This is usually worked *in situ*, into a circular space, although it can be used in an irregular space if you want to create an asymmetrical effect.

Divide your circle into eight sections by taking threads across to the opposite points. Whip the thread back along the last thread until you reach the middle. Begin weaving the web by taking your thread under two of the radiating threads and back over one; repeat this process all the way round. Carry on until you have filled in enough of the web to create the desired effect. Whip the thread along one of the radiating threads to the outside edge and fasten off. Work a cordonnette round this space in the normal way.

Horizontal Shading

This shading is worked over Corded Brussels stitch, using two needles. First if all decide which way the shading goes – light to dark or dark to light.

STAGE 1: Working from dark to light, work down the area in Corded Brussels until you want to introduce the shading. Thread a needle with the next lightest thread and fasten

to the right-hand side of your work; both needles are now on this side. *Corded Brussels stitch may now be worked from either side.*

STAGE 2: Take the paler thread across as a cord, wind round the cordonnet on the other side and leave. Take the original thread and work the stitches from right to left. Work three rows in this way.

STAGE 3: Change over so that the original colour becomes the cord and the paler colour is used for the stitches. Work three rows.

STAGE 4: Fasten off the original colour and use the paler colour for cord and stitches. Work three rows.

STAGE 5: Introduce a paler colour and repeat the process.

Vertical Shading

To produce vertical shading two needles are used and it is easier to have them working from opposite ends of the petal.

STAGE 1: Begin your petal in the usual way, working a shortened row along one side. It is necessary at this stage to have in mind some idea of the shading 'spikes' you wish to work; if you find this difficult to visualise, mark your lines of shading onto the petal with a pencil or pen that will not smudge.

STAGE 2: When you have worked one or two rows in the main colour and taken the cord back to the top of the petal, join in your other colour on the right-hand side at **c** (see diagram). Take a cord of your contrasting colour up to the point where shading is to start and work the stitches back along the row.

STAGE 3: Pin your contrast needle to one side and complete the top half of this row with the main colour, making sure that after your last stitch the thread is taken through the first stitch of the contrasting colour. Again, shorter rows will need to be worked to fill in the top half of the petal.

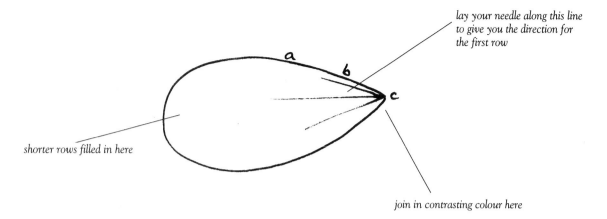

lay your needle along this line to give you the direction for the first row

a

b

c

shorter rows filled in here

join in contrasting colour here

vertical shading

Be careful to keep the rows as straight as you can so that your spikes of shading do not bend at the top. Do not work down to the point of the petal each time; only one row in three should be worked in this way, or there will be too much bulk at the bottom of the petal.

Short Rows

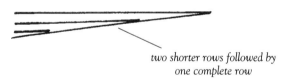

two shorter rows followed by one complete row

short rows

Having worked a full row of Corded Brussels, take the cord back towards the wider part of the petal and under the cordonnet, then work down to the point at which you want the shorter row to end. Take the cord back and work past the end of the short row, making sure that you work a stitch into the very last loop as you pass the place where the cord has hidden that loop. It is possible to fit two or three shorter rows in at one time, beginning with the longest short row and making them shorter as you work. *There is no need to take a cord down to the bottom each time because you already have one there.*

Lengthening a Row

lengthening a row – increasing

To lengthen a row, the thread is taken under the cordonnet to the place where the next row needs to begin. The first stitch of the next row is worked over this cordonnet with subsequent stitches being worked into the loops from the previous row as usual. If the row needs to be lengthened, the same process is repeated at each end. Sometimes more than one stitch needs to be added to increase the length; the extra stitches are always added over the cordonnet.

Increasing in the Middle of a Row

This can only be done successfully with Corded Brussels or a very close Single Brussels. Work your row of stitches normally until you want to increase. Put your needle into the next loop as if to make a stitch, but do not include the cord if working in Corded Brussels. Before completing the stitch, twist the needle

increasing in the middle of a row (1)

increasing in the middle of a row (2)

back into the previous loop (the one you have already worked into), this time incorporating the cord. Complete the stitch then work a stitch into that loop again.

Decreasing

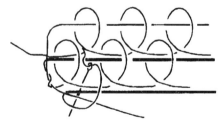

decreasing

To decrease in a very close stitch, simply miss out a loop where the stitches are beginning to crowd. To decrease at the end of a row, take your working thread through the first loop and out under the cordonnet without making a stitch, then complete the row in the usual way. The row may be shortened at its end, using the

same process. If you have reached the bottom of an area being filled, whip down the loops that meet the bottom cordonnet, thus shortening the row each time.

Working the Cordonnette

The general rule when working the cordonnette is to work the stitches to the outside of the curve. Having said that, rules are meant to be broken! A twisted cordonnette can be achieved by pulling your stitches up over the laid threads slightly each time so that edge travels over the top of the cordonnette. Various twists and patterns can be achieved using this method – it's up to you to experiment.

Beginning a Cordonnette
Extra threads are laid down on top of the cordonnet, usually two or four, but more if you need a thicker edging. Deal with these threads in exactly the same way as when laying the cordonnet; if two extra threads are being used, double a single thread and lay down the looped thread. Fasten your sewing thread to the beginning of the cordonnette to be worked; take the needle through the loop to fasten it, then work the cordonnette.

For a new section of cordonnette that butts up against an existing one, begin in the same way, but this time, when you take your needle through the loop, come through under the existing cordonnette and pull so that the loop disappears slightly. Take the needle back under the cordonnette ready to begin your work.

To Work a Continuous Cordonnette
Try to avoid cutting the threads. To work round a petal or leaf, decide first which part is in front of the other. If you need the shape to be complete, carry on the stitches in the same direction. Work up to the split, then put a pin in at the end of the shape. Wrap half the threads round the pin and back up to the split where your needle is waiting to work down over the laid threads. Having worked almost

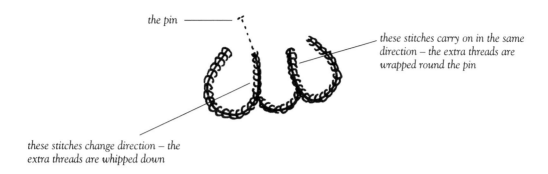

the pin

these stitches carry on in the same direction – the extra threads are wrapped round the pin

these stitches change direction – the extra threads are whipped down

working a continuous cordonnette

to the end, take out the pin, put your needle through the tiny loop to fasten, then take the needle in and out under the cordonnette until you are back at the split ready to carry on working.

When the next shape is in front of the one being worked, the stitches of the cordonnette need to change direction. Work down to the split, then whip half the threads down to the bottom of the shape; lay the threads back on

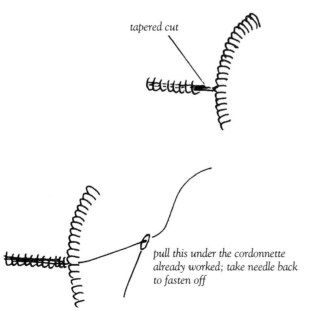

tapered cut

pull this under the cordonnette already worked; take needle back to fasten off

working the cordonnette

top of those whipped down. Your needle is at the bottom end by now, ready to work the stitches up towards and past the split.

Finishing a Cordonnette
When finishing off, work to within one or two stitches of the end, then cut the threads being laid down, but at an angle so that they are tapered towards the adjacent cordonnette. Work your last few stitches, being careful to encompass the ends that have been cut. Take your needle under the adjacent cordonnette and pull slightly; this will pull the one cordonnette so that it lies under the other.

A Raised Cordonnette

Using an ordinary cotton, make small bridge stitches over the section of cordonnet that is to be raised; these stitches graduate in width from small to large in the centre, then down to small again.

Use a thicker thread to pad out these stitches, leaving out the smaller bridge stitches as they become full, then leaving out the next two bridge stitches, and so on until all the stitches are padded out.

Work your cordonnette in the usual way over all the padding, making sure that your stitches lie close together and do not twist or overlap; this will give a smooth cordonnette.

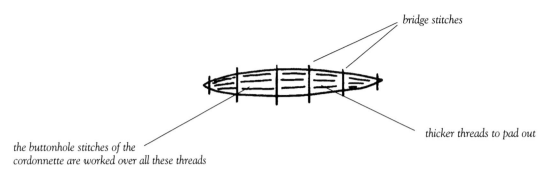

bridge stitches

thicker threads to pad out

the buttonhole stitches of the cordonnette are worked over all these threads

a raised cordonnette

Wall Pattern 1

All stitches are worked from left to right.

ROW 1: This is the foundation row.

CORD ROW: Take the cord back, whipping into the twelfth loop and every twelfth loop after that.

ROW 2: Work a stitch into each loop until you reach the one with the cord whipped in. Miss this loop; continue in the same way to the end of the row. (There should be ten loops between each hole.)

CORD ROW: Whip the cord into the loop on each side of the holes in the previous row.

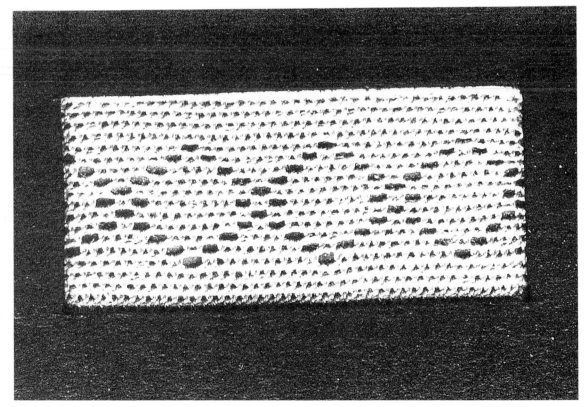

Wall pattern 1

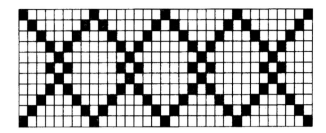

Wall pattern 1

ROW 3: Work stitches until you reach the loop before the hole; miss this loop and work two stitches into the hole on the previous row; miss the next loop then repeat to the end of the row (making seven loops between each hole).

CORD ROW: Whip the cord into the loops before and after the holes each time.

ROW 4: Work a stitch into each loop until you reach the one before the hole in the previous row. Miss this, work two stitches into the hole and miss the loop after the next hole. Continue to the end of the row (four loops between each hole).

CORD ROW: Whip into the loops before and after the holes each time.

ROW 5: Work as before; this time there will be only two stitches (one loop) between the holes at the point.

CORD ROW: Whip into the loop between the two holes.

ROW 6: Work a normal row, missing the whipped loop.

CORD ROW: Whip into the loop on each side of the hole.

ROW 7: Miss the loops that are whipped and worked two stitches into the hole in the previous row.

CORD ROW: Whip into the loop between the holes.

ROW 8: Work two stitches into each hole and miss out the whipped loop.

The next rows of the pattern are a repeat of rows 3 to 6.

This stitch can be used as a variation on Gros Point Diamonds and also as a filling.

Wall Pattern 2

ROW 1: This is a foundation row.

CORD ROW: Whip into the first loop and every twelfth loop after that.

ROW 2: Work this as a normal row, missing out the whipped loop each time (ten loops between each hole).

CORD ROW: Whip into the loop after the large one, then into the loop on each side of every large loop.

ROW 3: Work back, missing out the whipped loops and working two stitches into the large loop from the previous row (seven loops between each hole).

CORD ROW: Whip into the loop after the large one, then * whip into the loop before the hole and that after the next one. Repeat from * to the end of the row.

ROW 4: Work this row, missing out the whipped loops and replacing the stitches missed in the previous row (four loops between each hole).

Wall pattern 2

CORD ROW: Repeat the last corded row.

ROW 5: Work this row, leaving out the whipped loops and replacing the stitches missed in the last row (one loop between each hole).

CORD ROW: Whip into the loop before the first large loop, then the loop between and the loop after the next one; repeat to the end of the row.

ROW 6: Work this row, leaving out the whipped loops and working two stitches into the large loops of the previous row.

CORD ROW: Whip into the two loops between the three large loops; repeat to the end.

ROW 7: Leave the whipped loops and work two stitches into the large loops of the previous row.

CORD ROW: Whip into the loop between the two holes.

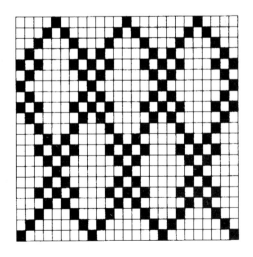

Wall pattern 2

ROW 8: Work back, missing the whipped loops and working two stitches into each hole.

CORD ROW: Whip into the loop on each side of the large loop; repeat.

ROW 9: Work back, missing out the whipped loops and working two stitches into the large loop in the previous row.

CORD ROW: Whip into the loop before the hole, then the loop between and that after the second large loop; repeat.

ROW 10: Work back, missing out the whipped loops.

Repeat rows from the cord row after row 3.

Wall Pattern 3

ROW 1: Work as a foundation row.

CORD ROW: Whip into every twelfth loop.

ROW 2: Work back, missing out the whipped loop each time.

CORD ROW: Whip into the loop on each side of the large loops.

ROW 3: Miss out the whipped loops and work two stitches into the large loops in the previous row.

CORD ROW: Whip into the loop before the large one and after the next large loop; repeat to the end of the row.

ROW 4: Work back, missing out the whipped loops and working two stitches into each large loop.

CORD ROW: Repeat the last cord row.

ROW 5: Repeat row 4.

CORD ROW: Whip into the loop between the two large loops, then into the fourth small loop; repeat to the end of the row.

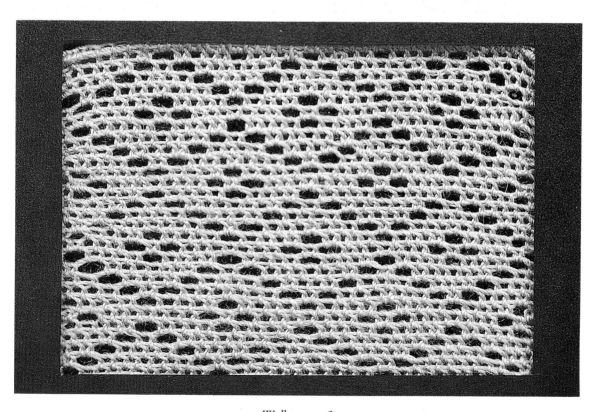

Wall pattern 3

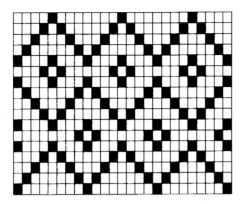

Wall pattern 3

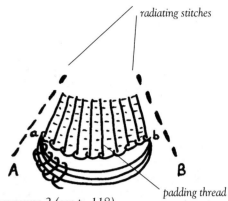

Flower couronne 2 (see p. 118)

ROW 6: Work this, missing out the whipped loops and working two stitches into each large loop. (You should now have a large loop at the tip of each 'v', plus one midway between them.)

CORD ROW: Whip into the loop on each side of the large loop in the middle of the inverted 'v'.

ROW 7: Work this, missing out the whipped loops and working two stitches into the large loop in the previous row.

CORD ROW: Whip into the small loop between the two large ones and then the fourth small loop after that; repeat to the end.

ROW 8: Repeat row 7. (You should now have a large loop under the point of the 'v' ready to repeat the pattern.)

CORD ROW: Repeat the pattern from the cord row before row 3.

Basic Couronne

STAGE 1: Use the corner of your base material and the thread you used for couching down the cordonnet. Make five stitches radiating out from a small centre circle and fasten off at the back of the material. The size of circle left in the middle determines the size of your finished couronne.

STAGE 2: Thread a needle with thicker thread

and run this under the stitches until the five radiating stitches have been filled, then cut off the end as closely as possible. You can use the same thread for both the padding and the couronne, in which case do not cut off the thread after padding but continue working the stitches.

STAGE 3: Using your normal working thread, take the needle under the ridge of thick thread until the end of your working thread is lost, then begin to buttonhole over all the threads. If you want to make to make a flat couronne, simply work round the circle, hook the thread into the edge of the first stitch and fasten off. If you wish to make a flower, add the petals as you work.

STAGE 4: Begin the buttonholing at one of the radiating stitches marked **A** in the diagram and count to the next radiating stitch (**B**). It will not be necessary to count if your radiating stitches are evenly spaced. Take your working thread back to the first stitch and thread through the tiny loop at the edge of the stitch. Now take the thread back to **b** then back to **a** again. Buttonhole over these three threads until you have reached **b** once more; this will give you a flower petal. Continue in this way, remembering to count the stitches in between each radiating stitch (unless you have spaced them evenly) so that the petals are the same distance apart.

These couronnes are stitched onto the work after it has been removed from its backing.

Couronnes: Variations on a Theme

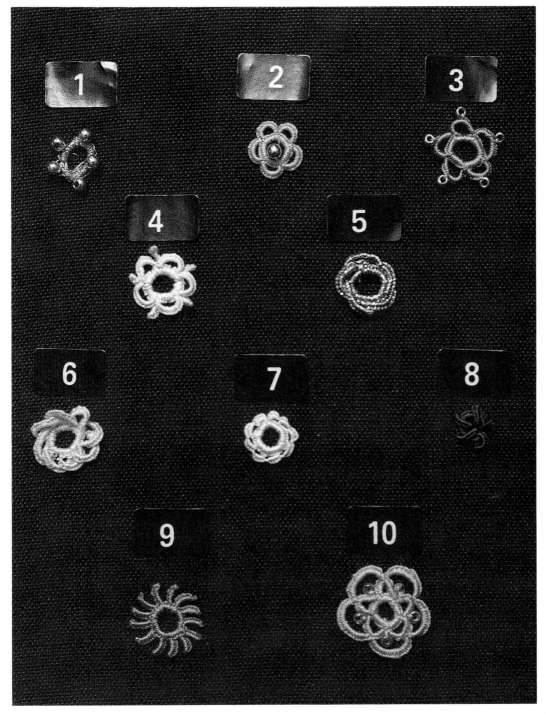

Couronnes worked by the author

COURONNE 1: Place five straight stitches onto your backing material; these should radiate out from a centre circle. Run a thicker thread under these stitches as explained in the previous section. Work a flat couronne by buttonholing all the way round but add a small bead at each of the radiating stitches.

COURONNE 2: Work a small flower couronne as explained in stage 4 of *Basic Couronne* (p. 116), but fill in the centre with small beads. You will have to sew these on afterwards.

COURONNE 3: Work a small flower couronne, this time adding a bead to the centre of each loop picot.

COURONNE 4: Lay down five straight stitches, radiating out from a centre circle with another straight stitch making a 'T' across the top of each radiating stitch. These small stitches are for the Venetian picots, one of which may be worked into each small stitch, either in the same colour as the main couronne or in a contrasting colour. The Venetian picots should be worked first, taking the thread round the circle under the other threads from picot to picot. Then work the couronne with looped picots in the usual way.

COURONNE 5: This couronne is also begun in the usual way. Work the first looped picot normally, then work round the main couronne until you are halfway between the end of the last looped picot and the next radiating stitch.

Work your next looped picot from here back to the centre of the last one. In this way you are overlapping the looped picots.

COURONNE 6: This couronne is worked in the same way as stage 5 but the looped picots are larger.

COURONNE 7: Work a flat couronne then work Cinq Point de Venise stitches round this couronne, working into the small loops at the edge of the buttonhole stitches.

COURONNE 8: Again work a flat couronne, then work a half-couronne over the original at each of the radiating stitches.

COURONNE 9: When you lay out your radiating stitches work a row of running stitches approximately ½ cm. from the inside circle. Work the main couronne and a Venetian picot into each running stitch; you should end up with a sunflower effect.

COURONNE 10: This is a normal 'small-flower' couronne with a bead worked in at the end of every looped picot and an extra row of loops. To work this extra row, begin in the middle of one of the existing loops and take the thread to the middle of the next loop, back to where you began. Repeat this process until you have four threads to buttonhole over. Buttonhole over these threads and this will take you to the end of a picot ready for the next one. N.B. You will have to have four threads to work over and not three as in the ordinary small flower. There are obviously numerous variations and combinations, and you'll enjoy trying out your own ideas. Experiment with

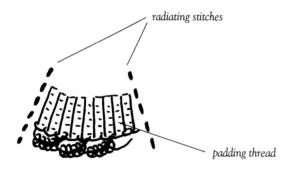

radiating stitches

padding thread

Flower couronne 7

wire round half the couronne

couronne incorporating wire (used in making the cow parsley for Waste Ground, see p. 81) more than one colour and more than one size of couronne; they can easily be built up one on top of the other, making an interesting centre for a piece of work.

Half-Couronnes

These are usually worked over an existing cordonnette. Having worked the cordonnette, take your needle behind it, loop round and behind it again. Do this until you have three or five loops over the cordonnette, then buttonhole over these loops.

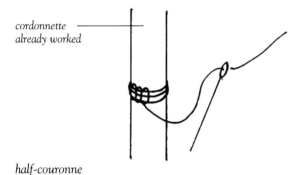

cordonnette already worked

half-couronne

To Make a Stumpwork Face

STAGE 1: Make a card template the size of the head you require. Place it on the cross-grain of a piece of soft calico. Draw round it and cut out, allowing an extra eighth of an inch all the round the edge. Run gathering stitches round the drawn line and pull up until the head is the size you want; fasten off.

STAGE 2: Stitch the head onto the background calico with stab stitches and a fine thread, beginning at the chin end and making sure the excess fabric is tucked underneath. Begin stuffing the head by pushing a tiny amount of wadding into the chin. Work your way up the face, making stab stitches alternately on each side and inserting more wadding as you go. When you reach the top of the head, put in the last lot of stuffing and sew up.

STAGE 3: Decide where the eyes should be,

then with a mid-brown colour make a stab stitch for each eye, taking your needle back at a 45° angle into the corner of the eye nearest the nose. This will give enough of an indentation on each side to create the impression of a nose; you can pinch it a little for emphasis. To make closed eyes, simply work a straight stitch for each eye; for an open eye, make two straight stitches for each eye and pull them apart with a small stab stitch each time. If you want to put eyebrows in, make a small straight stitch above the eye.

STAGE 4: Make a stab stitch for the mouth. An open mouth may be created in the same way as for the eye.

STAGE 5: The hair is made by working straight stitches in the chosen colour; small ringlets are made with Bullion knots. If you wish the ears to show, make these using a flesh coloured thread and Bullion knots: one small knot inside and a larger one for the outside.

To Make Stumpwork Hands

Take a piece of fine wire approximately 4 cm. long. Bind the middle 1 cm. of this and secure with a half-hitch. Use a pair of pincers to bend the bound piece in half. Bind the doubled and bound wire once again, leaving a small piece at the top to look like the fingernail. Repeat this four times so that you have four fingers and a thumb. Arrange these in the right order, then bind them together in a figure of eight, in and out between the fingers to begin with, then round all the fingers, putting in the little finger and thumb as you go. This binding will create the palm of the hand. Bend the fingers into the required shape.

How to Make a Cord

Choose two points to hook your thread on; for a long cord they need to be a good way apart, at least three or four yards, because the twist takes up the thread. Loop your thread backwards and forwards between these two points until you have three threads. Knot one end and leave it on the hook or with the person holding it. At the other end make another knot, then put a pencil inside the loop created; hold the threads on the other side of the pencil and twist the pencil until the thread is twisted all the way along. Put the two ends of the thread together and they will twist into a cord. If the cord is not tight enough, you need more twist at the beginning. This cord can then be cut to the lengths required, the ends knotted and sewn into place.

For a thicker cord, simply increase the number of threads between the two points when you begin. A shorter cord may be twisted between your fingers.

Book Suppliers

The following are stockists of the Batsford/Dryad Press range:

ENGLAND

AVON
Bridge Bookshop
7 Bridge Street
Bath BA2 4AS

Waterstone & Company
4-5 Milsom Street
Bath BA1 1DA

BEDFORDSHIRE
Arthur Sells
Lane Cover
49 Pedley Lane
Clifton
Shefford SG17 5QT

BUCKINGHAMSHIRE
J.S. Sear
Lacecraft Supplies
8 Hillview
Sherington MK16 9NJ

CAMBRIDGESHIRE
Dillons the Bookstore
Sidney Street
Cambridge

CHESHIRE
Lynn Turner
Church Meadow Crafts
7 Woodford Road
Winsford

DEVON
The Carey Company
75 Slade Close
Ottery St Mary EX11 1SY

Creative Crafts & Needlework
18 High Street
Totnes TQ9 5NP

Honiton Lace Shop
44 High Street
Honiton EX14 8PJ

DORSET
F. Herring & Sons
27 High West Street
Dorchester DT1 1UP

Tim Parker (*mail order*)
124 Corhampton Road
Boscombe East
Bournemouth BH6 5NZ

Christopher Williams
19 Morrison Avenue
Parkstone
Poole BH17 4AD

DURHAM
Lacemaid
6, 10 & 15 Stoneybeck
Bishop Middleham DL17 9BL

GLOUCESTERSHIRE
Southgate Handicrafts
63 Southgate Street
Gloucester GL1 1TX

Waterstone & Company
89-90 The Promenade
Cheltenham GL50 1NB

HAMPSHIRE
Creative Crafts
11 The Square
Winchester SO23 9ES

Doreen Gill
14 Barnfield Road
Petersfield GU31 4DR

Needlestyle
24-26 West Street
Alresford

Ruskins
27 Bell Street
Romsey

ISLE OF WIGHT
Busy Bobbins
Unit 7
Scarrots Lane
Newport PO30 1JD

KENT
The Handicraft Shop
47 Northgate
Canterbury CT1 1BE

Hatchards
The Great Hall
Mount Pleasant Road
Tunbridge Wells

LONDON
W. & G. Foyle Ltd
113-119 Charing Cross Road
WC2H 0EB

Hatchards
187 Piccadilly W1V 9DA

MIDDLESEX
Redburn Crafts
Squires Garden Centre
Halliford Road
Upper Halliford
Shepperton TW17 8RU

NORFOLK
Stitches and Lace
Cromer Road
Alby
Norwich NR11 7QE

Waterstone & Company
30 London Street
Norwich NR2 1LD

NORTH YORKSHIRE
Craft Basics
9 Gillygate
York

Shireburn Lace
Finkle Court
Finkle Hill
Sherburn in Elmet LS25 6EB

The Craft House
23 Bar Street
Scarborough YO13 9QE

SOMERSET
Bridge Bookshop
62 Bridge Street
Taunton TA1 1UD

STAFFORDSHIRE
J. & J. Ford (*mail order & lace days only*)
October Hill
Upper Way
Upper Longdon
Rugeley WS15 1QB

WARWICKSHIRE
Christine & David Springett
21 Hillmorton Road
Rugby CV22 6DF

WEST MIDLANDS
Needlewoman
21 Needles Alley
off New Street
Birmingham B2 5AG

WEST YORKSHIRE
Sebalace
Waterloo Mill
Howden Road
Silsden BD20 0HA

George White Lacemaking Supplies
40 Heath Drive
Boston Spa LS23 6PB

Just Lace
Lacemaker Supplies
14 Ashwood Gardens
Gildersome
Leeds LS27 7AS

Jo Firth
58 Kent Crescent
Lowstown, Pudsey
Leeds LS28 9EB

WILTSHIRE
Everyman Bookshop
5 Bridge Street
Salisbury SP1 2ND

SCOTLAND

Embroidery Shop
51 William Street
Edinburgh
Lothian EH3 7LW

Waterstone & Company
236 Union Street
Aberdeen AB1 1TN

WALES

Bryncraft Bobbins (*mail order*)
B.J. Phillips
Pantglas
Cellan
Lampeter
Dyfed SA48 8JD

Hilkar Lace Supplies
33 Mysydd Road
Landore
Swansea

Equipment Suppliers

UNITED KINGDOM

BEDFORDSHIRE
A. Sells
49 Pedley Lane
Clifton
Shefford SG17 5QT

BERKSHIRE
Chrisken Bobbins
26 Cedar Drive
Kingsclere RG15 8TD

BUCKINGHAMSHIRE
J.S. Sear
Lacecraft Supplies
8 Hillview
Sherrington MK16 9NJ

Winslow Bobbins
70 Magpie Way
Winslow MK18 3PZ

SMP
4 Garners Close
Chalfont St Peter SL9 0HB

CAMBRIDGESHIRE
Josie and Jeff Harrison
Walnut Cottage
Winwick
Huntingdon PE17 5PP

Heffers Graphic Shop (*matt coloured transparent adhesive film*)
26 King Street
Cambridge CB1 1LN

Spangles
Carole Morris
Cashburn Lane
Burwell CB5 0ED

CHESHIRE
Lynn Turner
Church Meadow Crafts
7 Woodford Road
Winsford

DEVON
Honiton Lace Shop
44 High Street
Honiton EX14 8PJ

DORSET
Frank Herring & Sons
27 High West Street
Dorchester DT1 1UP

T. Parker (*mail order, general and bobbins*)
124 Corhampton Road
Boscombe East
Bournemouth BH6 5NZ

ESSEX
Needlework
Ann Bartlett
Bucklers Farm
Coggeshall CO6 1SB

GLOUCESTERSHIRE
T. Brown (*bobbins*)
Temple Lane Cottage
Littledean
Cinderford

Chosen Crafts Centre
46 Winchcombe Street
Cheltenham GL52 2ND

HAMPSHIRE
Needlestyle
24-26 West Street
Alresford

Newnham Lace Equipment (*lace pillows*)
15 Marlowe Close
Basingstoke RG24 9DD

Richard Viney
Unit 7
Port Royal Street
Southsea PO5 3UD

ISLE OF WIGHT
Busy Bobbins
Unit 7
Scarrots Lane
Newport
PO30 1JD

KENT
The Handicraft Shop
47 Northgate
Canterbury CT1 1BE

Denis Hornsby
25 Manwood Avenue
Canterbury CT2 7AH

Francis Iles
73 High Street
Rochester ME1 1LX

LANCASHIRE
Malcolm J. Fielding (*bobbins*)
2 Northern Terrace
Moss Lane
Silverdale LA5 0ST

LINCOLNSHIRE
Ken and Pat Schultz
Whynacres
Shepeau Stow
Whaplode Drove
Spalding PE12 0TU

MERSEYSIDE
Hayes & Finch
Head Office & Factory
Hanson Road
Aintree
Liverpool L9 9BP

MIDDLESEX
Redburn Crafts
Squires Garden Centre
Halliford Road
Shepperton TW17 8RU

NORFOLK
Stitches and Lace
Cromer Road
Alby
Norwich NR11 7QE

George Walker
The Corner Shop
Rickinghall, Diss

NORTH HUMBERSIDE
Teazle Embroideries
35 Boothferry Road
Hull

NORTH YORKSHIRE
The Craft House
23 Bar Street
Scarborough

Shireburn Lace
Finkle Court
Finkle Hill
Sherburn in Elmet LS25 6EB

Stitchery
Finkle Street
Richmond

SOUTH YORKSHIRE
D. H. Shaw
47 Lamour Crescent
Rotherham S66 9QD

STAFFORDSHIRE
J. & J. Ford (*mail order and lace days only*)
October Hill
Upper Way
Upper Longdon
Rugeley WS15 1QB

SUFFOLK
A. R. Archer (*bobbins*)
The Poplars
Shetland
near Stowmarket IP14 3DE

Mary Collins (*linen by the metre, and made up articles of church linen*)
Church Furnishings
St Andrews Hall
Humber Doucy Lane
Ipswich IP4 3BP

E. & J. Piper (*silk embroidery and lace thread*)
Silverlea
Flax Lane
Glemsford CO10 7RS

SURREY
Needle and Thread
80 High Street
Horsell
Woking GU21 4SZ

Needlestyle
5 The Woolmead
Farnham GU9 7TX

SUSSEX
Southern Handicrafts
20 Kensington Gardens
Brighton BN1 4AC

WARWICKSHIRE
Christine & David Springett
21 Hillmorton Road
Rugby CV22 5DF

WEST MIDLANDS
Framecraft
83 Hampstead Road
Handsworth Wood
Birmingham B2 1JA

The Needlewoman
21 Needles Alley
off New Street
Birmingham B2 5AE

Stitches
Dovehouse Shopping Parade
Warwick Road
Olton, Solihull

WEST YORKSHIRE
Jo Firth
Lace Marketing & Needlecraft Supplies
58 Kent Crescent
Lowtown
Pudsey LS28 9EB

Just Lace
Lacemaker Supplies
14 Ashwood Gardens
Gildersome
Leeds LS27 7AS

Sebalace
Waterloo Mills
Howden Road
Silsden BD20 0HA

George White Lacemaking Supplies
40 Heath Drive
Boston Spa LS23 6PB

WILTSHIRE
Doreen Campbell (*frames and mounts*)
Highcliffe
Bremilham Road
Malmesbury SN16 0DQ

SCOTLAND
Christine Riley
53 Barclay Street
Stonehaven
Kincardineshire

Peter & Beverley Scarlett
Strupak
Hill Head
Cold Wells, Ellon
Grampian

WALES
Bryncraft Bobbins
B. J. Phillips
Pantglas
Cellan
Lampeter
Dyfed SA48 8JD

Hilkar Lace Suppliers
33 Mysydd Road
Landore
Swansea

AUSTRALIA

Australian Lace magazine
P. O. Box 609
Manly
NSW 2095

Dentelles Lace Supplies
c/o Betty Franks
39 Lang Terrace
Northgate 4013
Brisbane
Queensland

The Lacemaker
724a Riversdale Road
Camberwell

Spindle and Loom
Victoria 3124
83 Longueville Road
Lane Cove
NSW 2066

Tulis Crafts
201 Avoca Street
Randwick
NSW 2031

NEW ZEALAND

Peter McLeavey
P. O. Box 69. 007
Auckland 8

USA

Arbor House
22 Arbor Lane
Roslyn Heights
NY 11577

Baltazor Inc.
3262 Severn Avenue
Metairie
LA 7002

Beggars' Lace
P. O. Box 481223
Denver
Colo

Berga Ullman Inc.
P. O. Box 918
North Adams
MA 01247

Happy Hands
3007 S. W. Marshall
Pendleton
Oreg 97180

International Old Lacers Inc.
124 West Irvington Place
Denver
CO 80223–1539

The Lacemaker
23732-G Bothell Hwy, SE
Bothell
WA 98021

Lace Place de Belgique
800 S. W. 17th Street
Boca Raton
FL 33432

Lacis
3163 Adeline Street
Berkeley
CA 94703

Robin's Bobbins
RT1 Box 1736
Mineral Bluff
GA 30559-9736

Robin and Russ
   Handweavers
533 North Adams Street
McMinnville
Oreg 97228

The Unique and Art Lace Cleaners
5926 Delman Boulevard
St Louis
MO 68112

Unicorn Books
Glimakra Looms 'n Yarns Inc.
1304 Scott Street
Petaluma
CA 94954-1181

Van Sciver Bobbin Lace
130 Cascadilla Park
Ithaca
NY 14850

The World in Stitches
82 South Street
Milford
NH 03055

Sources of Information

UNITED KINGDOM

Guild of Needlelaces
Mrs June Dawkins (Chair)
Netherlea
39 Moor Road
Breadsall
Derby DE7 6AA

The Lace Guild
The Hollies
55 Audnam
Stourbridge
West Midlands DY8 4AE

The Lacemakers' Circle
49 Wardwick
Derby DE1 1HY

The Lace Society
Linwood
Stratford Road
Oversley
Alcester
War BY9 6PG

The British College of Lace
21 Hillmorton Road
Rugby
War CV22 5DF

Ring of Tatters
Miss B Netherwood
269 Oregon Way
Chaddesden
Derby DE2 6UR

United Kingdom Director of
    International Old Lacers
S. Hurst
4 Dollis Road
London N3 1RG

USA

International Old Lacers Inc.
124 West Irvington Place
Denver
CO 80223–1539

Lace & Crafts magazine
3201 East Lakeshore Drive
Tallahassee
FL 32312-2034

OIDFA
(International Bobbin and Needle
    Lace Organization)
Kathy Kauffmann
1301 Greenwood
Wilmette
IL 60091
USA

Index